Choose Hope

(Always Choose Hope)

To Beth,
    I always enjoy visiting
with you.

        Best Wishes,
            Betsy

ELIZABETH J. CLARK

ISBN 978-1-64003-194-4 (Paperback)
ISBN 978-1-64003-195-1 (Digital)

Covenant Books, Inc.
11661 Hwy 707
Murrells Inlet, SC 29576
www.covenantbooks.com

Contents

Preface

This book is intended as a resource for the person who is trying to find or hold on to hope. It is meant to help those who are struggling with adversity, illness, loss, and grief, and those who are in danger of becoming hope-lost.

My interest in hope began decades ago with my first job as a medical social worker in a hospital hematology/oncology unit. At that time, a diagnosis of cancer was often equated with a death sentence. Despite poor odds, I found that patients continued to hope and that their hopes changed as their situations changed. I watched people get discouraged with treatments and side effects, but I recall very few who gave up hope completely. Despite a life-limiting disease, hope remained.

Years later, I became involved with the cancer survivorship movement. Cancer therapies had advanced. Patients were not only living longer, but many were being cured of cancer. Psychosocial aspects of cancer, including the importance and impact of hope, were being studied.

For me, that period had both professional and personal impact. I had completed my doctoral degree in medical sociology with a dissertation focusing on how people adapted to a disease as devastating as cancer. Once again, I was struck by individual stamina, perseverance, and hopefulness.

On a personal level, cancer took on a new reality. My only sister, Eleanor, was diagnosed with multiple myeloma, a blood cancer that had very poor survival rates at that time. She was forty-one years old, and the odds were that she would not live to be forty-five. The news was devastating, but as a family that had weathered other crises, we were individually—and collectively—stoic, forward looking, and positive. My sister, with a college degree in mathematics, had always been practical and realistic. She understood the statistics and the probabilities, and she decided she could—and would— overcome many of them. She became a model of hope for our entire family and for many other cancer survivors.

Despite many challenges, setbacks, and disappointments, Eleanor outlived all of the medical predictions. She had multiple surgeries, chemotherapies, and radiation therapy. She developed a second cancer (uterine cancer) and successfully underwent treatment for that. A few months before she died, she was diagnosed with a leukemia that was related to treatments she had received over the years. Despite great effort on the part of her health-care team, she never achieved full remission of the leukemia. After months of hospitalizations and transfusions, she decided to stop all treatment and to manage her death as she had managed her life.

If asked, my sister would have told you that the thirteen years she lived with a cancer diagnosis were some of the best of her life, but I often wondered how Eleanor kept her hopes up. I know she struggled with pain and side effects.

Only once did I hear her question why she had gotten cancer. She worked at avoiding negative people, asking instead that family and colleagues be positive. She often used humor. For example, her oncologist could never simply relay good news. Instead, whenever he told her that she was in remission, he would add that she must remember that it was temporary, that she would go out of remission again at some point. She referred to him as Dr. Doom. I am certain he cared about her greatly and that he was only trying to be realistic, but it would have been nice to occasionally hear good news without any caveats.

There is one story about my sister that always inspires me. She knew her remissions were not lasting as long, and she knew they were not as strong. She decided it was time to reorganize her life. She had always wanted to see Alaska, so her final summer, she sold her house and booked us passage on an Alaskan cruise. One afternoon, we stopped at a small village that sold souvenirs and artwork made in Russia. There was a beautiful hand-painted barrette for sale. Eleanor looked at it several times. She knew she would probably face more chemotherapy (and hair loss) after the cruise. She bought it anyway. She only got to wear it for a few weeks, when, as expected, she had to start treatment again. That barrette symbolizes my sister's hope. I keep it near my desk, where I can see it each day.

Many, many families and individuals have similar stories of tragedy and sadness. They also have stories of overcoming adversity and coping with huge obstacles. The more I worked in the cancer field, the more I learned that my sister's story—her strength and perseverance—was much more commonplace than I had initially thought. What I came to realize was that hope is the key.

Hope is often misunderstood, and many people think that hope is the same as wishing or optimism. They believe that hope is a singular concept and that everyone hopes in the same way. We now know that people learn and use hope differently and that there are different types of hope. Hope can be for something general or something particular and specific. It can be grounded in religious or spiritual beliefs, formed by past experiences, or based on science or the outcome of therapy. Hope is like a kaleidoscope, changing as situations and circumstances change. With each turn of that kaleidoscope, you have a choice.

Always, always choose hope.

Elizabeth J. Clark

CHAPTER ONE

How Important Is Hope?

Hope is the pillar that holds up the world.
—Pliny the Elder

I s hope really necessary—for the individual, for the community, for the world? Throughout history, that question has been answered in the affirmative by philosophers, theologians, writers, mental health professionals, and national leaders.

By the thirteenth century, hope was considered to be a fundamental emotion. In the early sixteenth century, German theologian and Protestant religious leader Martin Luther noted the universal importance of hope when he stated, "Everything that is done in the world is done by hope." The French romantic writer and author of *Les Misérables*, Victor Hugo, claimed, "The word which God has written in the brow of every person is hope." German statesman and writer Johann Wolfgang von Goethe admonished, "In all things, it is better to hope than despair."

More recently, in his book *The Anatomy of Hope: How People Prevail in the Face of Illness*, physician Jerome Groopman emphasizes that there is an authentic biology of hope, and he concludes, "Hope, I have come to believe, is as vital to our lives as the very oxygen that we breathe."

Perhaps the spirit, breadth, and value of hope can be partially demonstrated by choosing hope when naming many of our home cities. For example, there are 102 places in the United States named Hope or that have *hope* as part of their name. An additional 13 are named New Hope. There is Hope, Alaska (population 192), a former gold-mining town, and Hope, Arkansas (population 10,004), where former President Bill Clinton was born. Hope, Arkansas, began in 1873 when a railroad was built through the area.

Places called Hope are not found only in the United States. There are 50 places in the world named Hope, and they are in a variety of countries from Canada to New Zealand to South Africa to Pakistan. Some countries have more than one town by that name. There are six towns called Hope in the United Kingdom and five in Jamaica.

Regardless of geographic location, it appears that town founders who chose names related to hope were forward looking and hopeful. They understood that hope included a vision of a future, and they saw their towns as having positive potential for overcoming adversity, even thriving.

The geography of hope helps us to realize that hope is recognized and used broadly. In addition, almost every language has a word for *hope*, and hope is found in all cultures. It has been depicted in ancient art, in great literature, and in every religion across millennia.

While hope is often a central tenet of religion, it is not a product of any one specific religion, nor is it confined to religious systems in general. However, to fully understand hope and its importance in modern culture, it is necessary to recognize hope's historical linkage to religion and to the symbolism, sacred and secular, that still holds meaning for us.

We also need to better understand the significance, utility, and power of hope in our everyday lives, in our communities, and in society. Hope is a valuable commodity, a renewable resource that helps us manage personal crises, find resolutions to far-reaching and seemingly entrenched problems at all levels of interaction, and plan for a desired and meaningful future.

The following chapters cover broad topics like how we define hope, learn to hope, and maintain hope even in the face of great adversity such as life-limiting illness and loss; how we prevent hopelessness and become hope bearers for our loved ones and our communities; how hope can be reclaimed after grief, whether experienced personally or professionally; and how hope can bring about needed social change and define an appropriate path forward. In each of these areas, there is an emphasis on hope as a choice and why it is important to always, always choose.

Hope Highlights

- History indicates hope is essential in our lives.
- Every language has a word for hope.

- Hope has been depicted in art and literature for millennia.
- Hope is a central tenet of religion, but it is not confined to religious systems.

CHAPTER TWO

Religious Roots of Hope

The sun set; but not his hope:
Stars rose; his faith was earlier up.
—Ralph Waldo Emerson

Much religious teaching has a basis in hope—hope for survival, hope for redemption, hope for salvation, hope for nirvana, hope for an eternal life, hope for the future. The 1828 edition of *Webster's Dictionary* noted this relationship between hope and religion in its definition for hope:

> Confidence in a future event; the highest degree of well founded expectation of good; as a hope founded on God's gracious promises; a scriptural sense.

The religion of the Old Testament could be called a religion of hope, and Christianity, Judaism, and Islam are rooted in the same tradition. In fact, in Christianity, the Bible is called "the Book of Hope," and depending on the version of the Bible used, the word *hope* is mentioned in over one hundred verses.

The Christian faith has its roots in the life and teachings of Jesus Christ. Religious scholar Roger Haight defines a Christian as "one whose faith in God is mediated through Jesus Christ." Christianity encompasses a diversity of doctrines and practices found among varied Christian groups such as Catholics, Protestants, and Orthodox Christians. Some of the essential Christian doctrines include belief in monotheism (only one God), the deity of Christ, the resurrection of Christ, salvation through grace, prayer, life after death, and the Gospels.

There are some notable differences. For example, one characteristic of Catholicism is the exalted worship of the Madonna. The pope is the visible head of the Catholic Church. Catholics also are the only group that recognizes the dogma of purgatory (an intermediate step between heaven and hell). There also are differences in the use of icons. The Orthodox Church has widespread use of icons, Catholics use some, but Protestants have few, if any.

Despite these differences, all three hold to the same basic essentials, and as noted in the Bible, hope is built on faith. This linkage of hope and faith is depicted in Hebrews (11:1): "Faith is confidence in what we hope for."

In Judaism, the Hebrew word for hope is *tikvah*, which means not only "hope," but "cord" and "expectation." The Hebrew root word means "to bind together (or collect)," and "to expect (or wait)." In this definition, hope is real, like grabbing onto a strong and secure rope. It also indicates patience, that one may have to wait for fulfillment. Hope then is an extension of faith. Psalm 71:5 states, "For thou art my hope [*tikvah*], O Lord God; thou art my trust from my youth."

In Islam, the religious faith of Muslims, the Holy Qur'an (also known as the Koran) emphasizes that hope is faith in Allah (Arabic word for Almighty God) and the hereafter (33:21), and that the foundation of hope is the good that we do in this life (47:35). It also teaches its followers to never lose hope that a situation will improve, that certain events are inevitable.

Hinduism, the world's third largest religion, is based mainly in India. It has numerous deities, spiritual processes, and philosophical traditions. Hinduism contains the tenets of dharma (experiential wisdom), karma (deeds and acts), the cycle of births and deaths for each soul, and liberation or nirvana. There are three ways to pursue the path of liberation: devotion, knowledge, or duty. Each individual has to find his or her own path, and the future is in the hands of the individual, so no change will come by hoping for the future. Reincarnation offers hope since the maturing of the soul takes many lifetimes. That means there will be great opportunity for learning and growing in future lives.

The religion of Native Americans, or First Nations People, represents the spiritual practices of the indigenous peoples of America. Their spirituality is closely and deeply connected to nature. They believe all things—life, nature, and spirit—are connected and united, and their beliefs, rituals, and symbols have been handed down, mainly by stories, from generation to generation.

The frequency with which the word *hope* is used in our everyday conversations shows the extent to which hope is part of our culture and its importance and high value in our society. There are numerous common phrases about hope, many of which have been drawn from religion, that have become part of our daily thinking and speech. Several of these phrases are used when we are feeling anxious or doubtful or disbelieving.

For example, "Hope against hope"—hoping for something even though there is little chance of succeeding—links back to Romans (4:18): "Who against hope believed in hope." "Cling to hope"—to hold onto hope regardless of the direness of the situation, or even though the chance of success is very small—is drawn from Hebrews (10:23, World English Bible): "Let us hold fast the confession of our hope without wavering, for he who promised is faithful." Another popular phrase, "There's no hope in hell that [some event] will occur," speaks to the bleakness and hopelessness of hell as described in both religious and classical writings. Almost everyone knows the line from Dante's *Inferno*, "Abandon hope all ye who enter here."

Some words are combined frequently with the word *hope*. For example, the three words *hope*, *peace*, and *joy* are often found together on holiday cards. These words are from Romans (15:13), "May the God of hope fill you with all joy and peace as you trust in him so that you may overflow with hope by the power of the Holy Spirit."

Hope also can be found as a frequent and comforting theme in hymns and other religious and spiritual songs. The Christmas song "O Holy Night," written in 1847, contains the phrase, "A thrill of hope, the weary world rejoices, for yonder breaks a new and glorious morn." This short line encompasses two essential components of hope: an expectation of achieving what is hoped for and desirability of the future.

"Whispering Hope," a hymn written by Septimus Winner in 1868, is still popular today. Its lyrics are based on Hebrews (6:18–20) which includes the phrase "to lay hold upon the hope set before us." The first verse states:

> Soft as the voice of an angel,
> Breathing a lesson unheard,
> Hope with a gentle persuasion
> Whispers her comforting word:
> Wait till the darkness is over,
> Wait till the tempest is done,
> Hope for the sunshine tomorrow,
> After the shower is gone.

People often find comfort in the words of this song, and many artists have performed it for a wide variety of audiences.

The hymn "Amazing Grace" was written in 1779 by Englishman John Newton. Newton had been working in the slave trade when he almost perished at sea during a storm. After that, he had a religious conversion and later became ordained as an Anglican clergyman. While different words have been added to the hymn since Newton wrote it, his original fourth stanza deals with the topic of hope:

> The Lord has promised good to me.
> His word my hope secures.

He will my shield and portion be;
As long as life endures.

It is estimated that "Amazing Grace" is performed over ten million times each year, and the words of the song have been translated into twenty-three languages.

Finally, whether or not an individual participates in organized religion or believes in any higher deity, most people recognize the hopeful and most popular psalm in the Bible, the Twenty-Third Psalm:

> The Lord is my shepherd; I shall not want. He maketh me to lie down in green pastures: he leadeth me beside the still waters. He restoreth my soul: he leadeth me in the paths of righteousness for his name's sake. Yea, though I walk through the valley of the shadow of death, I will fear no evil: for thou art with me; thy rod and thy staff they comfort me. Thou preparest a table before me in the presence of mine enemies: thou anointest my head with oil; my cup runneth over. Surely goodness and mercy shall follow me all the days of my life: and I will dwell in the house of the Lord for ever.

This psalm of David is one of the most loved literary works in the world. Written by King David, one of the earliest kings of Israel, it is revered by both Jews and Christians. Through millennia, the Twenty-Third Psalm has been used to comfort those facing challenges and going through difficult times, those who are ill, and those who are dying or grief-stricken. The beautiful words can calm souls and convey hope.

Hope Highlights

- In the Biblical religions, hope is built on faith.
- In Hinduism, reincarnation offers hope.
- Native American spirituality is based on nature.
- Hope is a part of our everyday culture.

CHAPTER THREE

Symbolism and Hope

We have this hope as an anchor of the soul,
both sure and steadfast.
—Hebrews 6:19

Along with written scriptures, oral histories, and music lyrics, great religious symbolism surrounds hope. The word *symbol* in Old Greek means "a throwing together." Today we think of a symbol as something material representing something abstract. A good example is the anchor, with its cross structure, that can be found throughout the Bible as the symbol of hope.

The dove is another religious symbol. The book of Genesis (8:8–12) describes the well-known story of Noah and the ark. According to the scriptures, after the flood, Noah released a dove to see if the waters were subsiding. When the dove finally returned with a freshly plucked olive leaf, Noah knew the flood was over and that land could be found. Today the dove is recognized as a symbol of hope and peace.

In addition to the dove, the story of Noah includes the rainbow that God placed in the sky as a covenant for continuity, a promise to never destroy the world by flood again. The rainbow, scientifically a meteorological event that occurs when the sun shines through raindrops, has been a religious symbol for centuries. People today still express awe when they see a single (and especially a double) rainbow.

Angels as Sacred Symbols

Angels have been the subject of sacred stories and major works of art for centuries, and are considered religious symbols for cultures around the world. Angel images were found in art as long as 2,500 years ago. The goddess Isis, a human figure with wings, appeared in Egyptian culture before the Christian era. The Greeks had a similar winged figure called Nike (around 500 BC). The Roman culture adapted the Nike figure, and the Christian Church continued the Greek and Roman imagery.

There are beautiful angel paintings by famous artists in classical art. *Madonna with Angels* by Filippo Lippi (1465), *Madonna on the Rocks* by Leonardo da Vinci (1506), and *The Archangel Leaving the Family of Tobias* by Rembrandt (1637) are three well-known examples.

Muslims also honor angels, and belief in angels is one of their fundamental articles of faith. While angels are considered to be real, Muslims believe they are made of light. As a result, there are few graphic representations of angels found in Islam art.

In many religions and cultures, angels are thought to be messengers of both hope and joy. In fact, in the original

Greek, *angelos* means "messengers," as does the Hebrew word *malach*. In Arabic, angels are called *mala'ika*, which means "to assist and keep." Angels are believed to communicate divine messages to humans and to possess great powers given to them by God or Allah or the Great Spirit. According to the Islam faith, the angel Gabriel brought down the Qur'an to the prophet Muhammad.

Native Americans refer to spiritual guides. They believe each person has a main protector guide, sometimes referred to as a gatekeeper spirit guide, who is always there to guide and protect their charge. Some tribes believe each person has two guides instead of only one.

Most people know the concept of guardian angels. Found in Christianity, Judaism, and Islam, and supported by the scripture in each, the major function of guardian angels is to protect individuals from harm, to guide and nurture them. Perhaps this concept is best described by a verse from Psalms (91:11), "For he shall give his angels charge over thee, to keep you in all thy ways." In the Catholic Church, October 2 has been celebrated as the Feast of the Guardian Angels since 1608.

France has a gold angel coin designed in 1792 by Augustine Dupré that is known throughout the world as an emblem of luck and protection. Most countries also have postage stamps that contain angel artwork. Yugoslavia issued one of the first, an Angel of Peace stamp, in 1919. In 1956, Vatican City issued a stamp with the Archangel Gabriel. In 1990, Lithuania issued a set of stamps, called Angelos, which depicted an angel safeguarding their country. In the United

States, the first angel Christmas stamp appeared in 1963, and other angel stamps have appeared in subsequent years.

In addition, in numerous countries around the world, angel depictions and statuary are found engraved on tombstones and standing in cemeteries. These frequently represent guardian angels still watching over a loved one who has died. The image of an angel protecting oneself or loved ones in life, as well as in death, is comforting. Many people, therefore, consider replicas and pictures of angels to be meaningful and sacred symbols of hope for them.

Stars as Symbols

Some of today's important religious symbols, like the six-pointed Star of David (also known as the Shield of David in Hebrew), are not referenced in the Bible or Talmud. The Star of David was adopted later in Jewish history, and has been used as the symbol on the flag of Israel since 1948. It is considered a symbol of unity, protection, and hope for Jews. Some people see the Star of David as two interlocking triangles. Others interpret it as representing the universe in all directions—north, south, east, west, zenith, and nadir, indicating that all are under God's sovereignty.

The Star of David is similar to the Hindu symbol called Shatkona, or the Star of Goloka, the eternal home of the Hindu deity Krishna. In addition, many Islamic mosques and artifacts contain the Star of David, although it is more often associated with the Seal of Solomon (named for biblical King Solomon who became king in 967 BC and ruled for forty years). Similarly, there is a star-shaped hexagram called the Kagone Crest which is found on many of the oldest Shinto shrines in Japan. Most experts believe the Kagone Crest has a cultural connection to the Shatkona of Hinduism rather than the Star of David.

One Native American symbol, called the "hope symbol," is an eight-pointed star surrounded by an unbroken circle. Roundness is often a metaphor for wholeness, indicating that all is contained within. In this imagery, the circle is a sign of protection. The star is actually composed of two smaller but connected stars. The inner star has four points signifying north, south, east, and west. The outer star also has four points. These represent the spring and fall equinoxes and the summer and winter solstices, each depicting hope for the future. Sometimes this symbol is referred to as "star knowledge" because its meaning is based on celestial alignments.

The hope star is closely related to Native American spiritual beliefs. The nineteenth century chief of the Duwamish Tribe, Chief Seattle, was known for his wisdom, and his words are often quoted, "Every part of the earth is sacred. We are part of the earth and it is part of us."

Secular Symbols of Hope

Symbols are not only drawn from religion. Many hope symbols are linked to cultures, groups, or causes. For example, Native American symbols can hold different meanings depending on the nation, tribe, and geographic location, and there are many Native American symbols related to hope.

Among these is a butterfly that is linked to self-transformation. In Native American culture, such symbols are used to decorate clothing and other personal items.

The state flag of Rhode Island is called the "hope flag." Its design was adopted in 1897. It depicts an anchor (symbol of hope) and a blue banner with the word *hope* written below. The anchor and banner motif is surrounded by thirteen stars representing the original thirteen colonies. Rhode Island was the thirteenth state to adopt the Constitution of the United States.

Poets, philosophers, writers, and artists all depict hope in their own medium and in their own way. One beautiful example of hope in modern art is a sculpture called *The Hope Tree* that sits in the lobby of the Martin O'Neil Cancer Center at Saint Helena Hospital in Saint Helena, California.

Created by Carol Jeanotilla, a sculptress who also has a nursing background, the metal tree stands thirteen feet high and eight feet wide, and weighs over three thousand pounds. Most significantly, embedded in the tree are forty-eight symbols representing images of hope from around the world.

Another beautiful depiction of hope called the Butterfly Garden of Hope can be found in Syracuse, New York. Cleverly landscaped into the shape of a large butterfly, it is a hope symbol drawn from nature. While it serves as a memorial to those who have died, it also functions as a symbol of hope for the living and a place of comfort for the grieving. It was developed by a nonprofit community agency that provides services for the bereaved.

Many organizations use symbols to brand their causes. Since 1957, cancer groups around the world (including the

American Cancer Society) have used the daffodil as their symbol of hope. Other groups use butterflies, rainbows, a stylized logo, or colored ribbons, the best known of which is the pink ribbon for breast cancer research. These symbols are a way of sending a message, of making hope a recognizable concept.

Symbols are not necessarily a source of hope, but they can be powerful reminders about the existence and importance of hope, and they can change how we think and look at the world. Symbols can be a representation of some future reality and can have a positive effect every time we see them.

We all know friends and family members who carry a lucky talisman—a coin or a charm or religious symbol—or who follow elaborate rituals and wear a special item of clothing when rooting for a favorite sports team. Others talk about lucky or significant numbers and use them at games of chance like playing the lottery. These are symbols for luck, most not based on fact or history, yet people strongly believe in them.

Think of how much more powerful symbols of hope are. They are grounded in religions or spirituality or cultures and have endured through the ages. Like the hymn mentioned previously, they convey a message of hope. Listen carefully to the message the symbol holds, and let it help you find and maintain your hope.

Hope Highlights

- Symbols are powerful visuals, and symbols representing hope abound.
- You can find symbols of hope in many places—in religious or spiritual teachings, in nature, and in art, music, and poetry.
- Symbols can change how you think about the world around you and can have a positive psychological impact.
- If a symbol has deep meaning for you, if it conveys a message of hope, keep it where you can see it frequently.

CHAPTER FOUR

Defining Hope: What Is Hope Anyway?

Everything can be taken from a man except to choose one's attitude in any given set of circumstances.
—Viktor Frankl

Previous chapters have discussed the historical and religious roots of hope and the sacred and secular symbols of hope. You may be wondering how hope is defined. Is there a clear definition? Part of the difficulty in defining hope is because *hope* is both a noun and a verb. That means hope is both a belief and a skill.

When *hope* is used as a noun, it indicates an object, something almost tangible. We speak about finding hope, losing hope, keeping hope, destroying hope, or taking hope away. Hope, then—my hope and your hope—is a prized possession. As a verb, though, hope requires action. If used as a transitive verb, it requires an object or goal. We are hoping for something or to accomplish or achieve something.

Hope researchers describe hope (when used as a noun) as an emotion—a complex emotion—like love, anger, or fear. It is a powerful individual emotion, one that helps us prevent despair and sustains us in times of stress and uncertainty. Hope can be an antidote to fear and a coping mechanism, or as one theorist noted, "Hoping is coping."

One of the best things about hope as an emotion is that it is an infinite resource. Like love, we have an endless supply. It is a renewable commodity. What hope we use today can be replenished tomorrow. Even if temporarily broken, our hope can be repaired, and full-bodied hope can be reestablished.

We are born with the capacity to hope, but the way we hope is a learned behavior. Children, for example, learn goal-directed thinking from examples set by the important people in their lives. Hope also is part of the wisdom passed from one generation to another, and family stories teach us the value and utility of hope. In addition to how our family of origin hopes, hope is influenced by our culture, our education, and our life experiences. This emphasizes that each person's hope is subjective, that one person's concept of hope is different from that of someone else, even different from the definition of hope held by family members and friends.

When used as a verb—to hope, hope that, or hope to do—a useful definition is that *hope is a way of feeling, thinking, and acting.* In this regard, hope also becomes a skill that can be mastered, strengthened, and used frequently.

Because most of us have never thought much about how we hope or the meaning that hope holds for us, we simply assume that everyone hopes the same way we do. Instead, what hope means for you, what you hope for, and what you do to act on that hope is intensely personal. This explains why no one can define hope for another person.

What Hope Is Not

Sometimes it seems easier to explain what hope is not rather than what hope is. It is not wishing. It is not optimism. It is not prayer. Each of these has its place, but none is the same as hope.

The word *hope* itself comes from the Latin word *cupio*, which means "to desire or wish well." Yet almost two hundred years ago, hope was distinguished from wishing. The 1828 *Webster's Dictionary* defined *hope* as "a desire of some good, accompanied with at least a slight expectation of obtaining it, or a belief that it is obtainable. Hope differs from wish and desire in this, that it implies some expectation of obtaining the good desired, or the possibility of possessing it." This definition is reinforced by the Old English word for hope, *hopa*, meaning "confidence in the future." Similarly, the Greek and Hebrew equivalent words for hope mean "confident expectation."

One major feature, then, that distinguishes hope from wishing, has to do with the probability of attainment, of obtaining specific goals. Wishing also lacks two other critical components of hope—action and reality orientation. Hope is always based in reality. It is not simply wishful or magical thinking.

Optimism is not hope. Optimism is an attitude. Like wishing, it is a way of thinking, but it includes only positive thinking. It puts the best face on any situation. The glass is always half-full, never half-empty. It is a generalized belief in good outcomes and a way of distancing an individual from anything negative. As such, optimism does not lead to planning or action.

People are often more optimistic in their expectation than is warranted by a situation. Sometimes an especially optimistic person is referred to as a "Pollyanna," a concept based on a best-selling children's book written by Eleanor Porter in 1913. The main character, Pollyanna, sees only the good side of any bad thing that happens to her. Optimism may close off any negative feelings and may result in inflexibility since only positive factors are considered.

There is nothing wrong with being optimistic, but optimism is not powerful like hope is. Optimism does not demand action, while hope is never passive. Hope requires goal-directed thinking to help individuals broaden their perspective and find routes or pathways to reach their goals.

Prayer also differs from hope. Praying presupposes a belief in God or some deity. It is a spiritual communication that can be in the form of praise, gratitude, confession, or a request for assistance or mercy. It also can be a form of an earnest wish. While prayer is not the same as hope, hope can be woven into prayer, and a person may pray to find or have adequate hope. For many people, praying amplifies hope by providing connection, understanding, strength, and support.

Hope Research

Research may help to clarify what sets hope apart. One of the foremost hope researchers, Richard Snyder, when defining hope, developing a theory of hope, and determining ways to measure hope, described hope as active and as requiring three essential elements—goals, willpower, and waypower. A goal is what you desire to do or to have. Waypower (pathways) is defined as "the perceived capability to find routes to your goals." Willpower (also referred to as agency) is the driving force, the total amount of energy you can summon to work toward your goals.

Twenty-five years ago, researchers James Averill, George Catlin, and Kyam Koo Chon, in their important studies on hope, put forth four overarching rules, or guiding principles, for hope that remain relevant today. Their "Rules of Hope" are:

- Prudential rules that place an emphasis on realism. Hope should be prudent and reasonable—the uncertainties should not be too great.
- Moralistic rules are related to a person's system of values. Whatever is hoped for should be both personally and socially acceptable.
- Priority rules concern the importance of the objects of hope. What a person hopes for should be of sufficient importance or vital interest.
- Action rules indicate that people who hope should be willing to take action to achieve their goals.

As hope research has advanced over the past fifty years, the concept of hope has been further and further refined. We now believe hope can be measured, examined, taught, and enhanced. We believe it can transform leadership, strengthen our communities, and impact illness and well-being. Subtypes of hope also help us understand hope more fully.

Subtypes of Hope

Hope is frequently divided into the three major types of hope—general hope, particular hope, and religious or spiritual hope. Today we also speak about therapeutic and broken hope. Frequently, the literature speaks of a category known as false hope; however, as noted below, hope can never be false.

Generalized Hope

Generalized hope is sometimes called trait or basic hope because it refers to a person's usual or characteristic level of hope. It is a general outlook or a character trait that includes a sense of the future. It also refers to a person's inner experience of hope and to a person's predisposition to hope. It is broad in scope. An example might be that someone hopes to maintain personal strength rather than give in to despair, or another hopes for overall motivation to carry on.

Particularized Hope

Particularized hope is directed hope or goal-directed thinking at a given moment. Sometimes described as state hope, it is the expectation of a significant future outcome that is focused on a particularly valued goal. In this type of hope, you are hoping for something. Maybe the desired outcome is finishing therapy, or being able to go on a family vacation, or getting pregnant, or feeling well enough to enjoy your twenty-fifth wedding anniversary.

Transcendent Hope

Transcendent hope is hope for meaning or for living with meaning. It is usually thought of as hope based on religion or spirituality, but neither is required to find meaning and purpose in life or in suffering. It involves our inner self and our identity. The word *transcendent* is derived from the Latin *transcentia*, meaning literally "to climb over." This type of hope extends beyond the limits of ordinary experience, our material existence, or the universe.

Therapeutic Hope

Therapeutic hope is a fairly recent conceptualization of a hope subtype that has gained in importance as our medical therapies have advanced. It is hope linked almost exclusively to the outcome of therapy. Health-care professionals are trained to be goal directed, and their goal is treating patients and curing or arresting disease. As a result of this focus, they may not fully understand or recognize the breadth of a patient's hope, or they may overlook the fact that for the patient there is hope beyond therapeutic hope.

A disappointment in treatment outcome or a lack of further therapeutic hope does not necessarily or immediately cause hopelessness for a patient. Maintaining hope, however, may depend at least partially on how the outcome is conveyed.

Broken or Lost Hope

The concept of broken hope first appeared in the literature fifty years ago when psychologist Ija Korner published an article titled "Hope as a Method of Coping." Up until that time, hope had largely been ignored by mental health practitioners. Korner declared that the purpose of hope was to guard against despair. Further, broken hope was attributed to a loss of faith or a breakthrough of doubts or a loss in what Korner called the "rationalizing chain." This presumed that people facing acute stress, failure, or major disappointment ended up losing their hope, thus becoming "hope-lost."

Today, many theorists might argue that hope is not simply lost; instead, it is taken away by an event that happens suddenly or by something that is said—often unintentionally. Sometimes the phrase *dashed hopes* is used to describe hope that has been destroyed. This phrase too is adapted from the Bible. Psalm 119:116 states, "Sustain me according to your promise and I will live; do not let my hope be dashed."

Hope is multifaceted and complex. While hope carries no assurance of success, it does contain a vision for a future yet to come. Hope helps us recognize possibilities, and it allows us to create our own futures. It is all of these things, but it can never be false.

The Impossibility of False Hope

"I don't want to give you false hope." Almost all of us have heard that phrase at some time, usually made by someone attempting to help us manage our expectations. What these individuals do not understand or recognize about hope is that hope is always reality based. There can be false reassurances, but not false hope. It is important to keep two things in mind.

First, by definition, hope can never be false. False hope is no more possible than false truth. It is an oxymoron, a contradiction of terms. Second, no matter how bleak a situation seems, there is always something to hope for, and no one should ever tell you a situation is hopeless.

Hope is flexible. It can change as situations and circumstances change. If a person's hope cannot be realized, a reformulation or reframing of that hope becomes necessary and new goals must be set. When faced with sudden turnings or setbacks, hope requires a transformation, a movement along the hope continuum. Quite often, new hopes can be found in the remnants of the old ones.

For example, at the time of a serious medical diagnosis, a person may begin by hoping for a cure. If that is not possible, hope may shift to hope for long-term survival or to meet some specific milestone. What we tend to forget is that even in serious and desperate situations, individuals can—and do—find hope. They are not immobilized by hopelessness, but they assess the changed situation and then determine further action.

Granted, some individuals can do this better than others. This may be related to their ability to be flexible or their problem-solving capabilities or to whether they generally have high or low hope.

Measuring Your Level of Hope

Hope researchers have spent years developing ways to measure someone's capacity for hope. They have developed scales that are now publicly available, easy to use, and fairly easy to understand.

Early hope researcher and nurse Mary L. Nowotny developed one of the first hope scales. She identified six critical attributes that must be present for an individual's hope to be measured:

- Hope is future oriented.
- Hope includes active involvement by the individual.
- Hope comes from within the individual and is related to trust.
- That which is hoped for is possible.
- Hope relates to other people or a higher being.
- The outcome of hope is important to the individual.

Another early hope scale is the Hope Index Scale published in 1982 by Obayuwana and colleagues. It is a sixty-item instrument for the objective assessment of hope in adults. The index is based on various surveys that identified five sources of what Obayuwana refers to as human hope:

> Human hope... is brought about as a result of ego strength (or intrinsic assets); perceived human family support (or human family assets); material sufficiency (or economic assets); level of knowledge, expertise, and experience (or educational assets); and spiritual awareness (or religious assets).

Other well-known hope researchers have developed separate hope scales for adults and children. If you wish, you can determine your hope baseline and track your progress toward becoming a more hopeful person. The scales also can help you better understand your level of hope and can indicate whether you are a high-, moderate-, or low-hope individual. Both high- and low-hope individuals can be successful and meet their hope goals. They may, however, use different methods for both goal setting and for determining hope strategies. In addition, high-hope individuals may be more flexible in their thinking and may view their goals more like challenges than threats. They also may set higher goals than low-hope individuals. Certainly, not everyone falls in the high-hope category, but as noted previously, hope and strategies for hope can be learned and modified. (See notes section for information on accessing various hope scales.)

Hope Highlights

- Hope has numerous subtypes.
- There is no such thing as false hope.
- Your hope level can be measured and enhanced.
- No matter how hard, always choose hope.

CHAPTER FIVE

Maintaining Personal Hope in Difficult Times

There never was night that had no morn.
—Dinah Murlock Craik

Hoping is a process, and hope is not always easy to maintain. It can become so fragile that an inadvertent comment or action can cause your hope to plummet. For example, if you were expecting good news about a medical issue, and instead of progress, things remain unresolved or became more negative, you might find your hope quickly diminishing.

If your hope runs low, you will need to replenish it. Where can you find new hope and how can you build on it? Start by thinking about what hope means for you and from where you generally draw hope—from within, from others, from a higher power, from nature? The kaleidoscope of hope is made up of many pieces, and a slight shift can change the total picture. A caring word, a small success, or a kind gesture may improve the outlook considerably.

Unexpected Hope

You may come across hope in surprising places and at surprising times. You could hear a speaker at a community event or on television who has a hopeful message that resonates with you. A chance conversation with a friend, or even a stranger, can help you put your hope in better perspective. While hope often appears unexpectedly, you may come across more hope if you are open to it and are constantly on the lookout for signs of hope.

Religion and Spirituality

If you use a religious framework for hope, visiting a church, synagogue, mosque, or another religious institution, or having a conversation with a member of the clergy can be hope-inspiring. Religious passages, religious rituals, or prayer also help some individuals maintain hope. Many people find the idea of a creating a sacred space an attractive idea. Well-known theologian and therapist Thomas Moore suggests a soul retreat. This may be a physical place you visit in order to get away from the problems of the world and everyday life. It should help restore or fill your soul. In a similar fashion, meditation can be a valuable activity for those seeking hope or trying to manage a personal crisis. Still others seek and find spiritual meaning, even sacredness, in daily life, and in important personal objects such as collections of special letters, photographs, or family mementos.

Friends

If you draw strength and hope from others, you may need to be selective when discussing your hope. It is not especially difficult to discern when someone's level of hope about your situation differs from your own. If it is at a higher level, it can bolster and multiply your own hope. When it is lower, it can have a negative, even disastrous, effect on your hope. When you are trying your best to hold on, to look forward with hope, the last thing you need is someone else suggesting that you lower your hopes. They may use hope-draining phrases like "I don't want you to get your hopes up." What you really need is more, not less, encouragement and hope. You need hope inspiration.

Support Groups

Attending a support program with individuals facing a situation like you are facing can be helpful, both to you as well as to the other group members. Similar challenges and suggestions for possible strategies and solutions can provide new ways of thinking. Positive personal stories can also be powerful antidotes to low hope when you are trying to overcome adversity, manage stress, or cope with loss. However, there are a few things to guard against. Make certain the group you choose to attend is forward thinking, hope enhancing, and offers nonjudgmental support. When you are trying to maintain hope, it is not helpful to be overwhelmed by the suffering and sadness of others or to be made to feel guilty or uncomfortable about your own hope level. Second, be selective about what you disclose, at least until you are sure that the support group is the right fit for you, and that what is discussed in the group meetings will be considered and remain confidential.

Journaling

It is a popular trend for people to keep a daily gratitude journal and enter several things each day for which they are grateful. This helps them keep a more positive perspective. If you find journaling enjoyable or useful, try including notes about hope on a regular basis. These can be encouraging words from others, things you have read, poetry, hopeful pictures, or simply noting that spring has arrived. If you make an entry or two each day, your hope list will grow, and it can become a permanent reminder of how important it is to maintain your hope. It is also helpful to jot down any random hopeful thoughts that cross your mind.

Self-Talk

Journaling can help make you aware of your self-talk, the things—positive and negative—you say to yourself during your waking hours. Earlier we noted that children learn what they live, and negative self-talk is learned from the messages received in childhood from family members, teachers, and even friends. (For example, "Oh Johnny, why can't you ever do things right?" or "I'm afraid you will never be good in math," or "You're such a crybaby.") These messages may have become so ingrained that you carried them with you into adulthood, and they still influence your self-talk. Self-talk has a serious impact on finding and maintaining hope. To overcome negative self-talk, you must be aware of it and you must work hard to change the messages you are sending yourself. Make certain your messages are as encouraging and uplifting as they can possibly be. Write them down if necessary. When you hear yourself saying something negative—whether out loud or in your head—stop the message immediately. Replace it with a positive message that supports your goals, helps you take action, and enhances your hope.

Practicing Hope

While you are at it, practice hope so that when times get difficult, you will have more hope available. Regularly, speak words of hope to yourself. Repeat them often. Make them your own mantra of hope. Remind yourself of times in the past when something seemed formidable—even hopeless—

and recall what helped you prevail. What strengths, skills, and conviction were available to you then, and how can they help you now? You may not feel hopeful at this very moment, but you can feel hopeful again.

Stockpiling Hope

Read hopeful articles, uplifting novels, or self-help books. Watch hopeful programs and movies, and keep a collection of programs and skits that make you laugh or make you happy. Put together a playlist of uplifting songs, and play them whenever you feel your hope slipping or when you need encouragement. Great athletes do this all the time. In the last Olympics, many of them listened to a piece of meaningful music or words of encouragement until the moment they had to participate in their event. Discuss hope with friends. Ask them how they define and maintain hope. Ask them about the most hopeful person they know and why they think that person is so hopeful. Volunteer for a day at a soup kitchen or food pantry, or attend a fundraising event for veterans or needy children. In addition to stockpiling hope for your own use in the future, you may find that you become a source of hope for someone else. Hope is contagious. Pass it on.

Nature and the Outdoors

Often individuals seek hope in nature. In spring, the first pussy willow, daffodil, or robin lifts their spirits. Seeing a new fawn or the colors of fall can be encouraging. Others find meaning and hope in natural phenomena like rainbows, stars, forests, and oceans. If nature is important to you, try to get outdoors and visit favorite spots every chance you can. Something as simple as walking outside right before dawn and watching the sun replace a dark night may be enough of a hope enhancer to help you get through a difficult day. Cut flowers in a vase can remind you of the beauty of life, or poring over catalogs and planning for a garden in the spring can keep you looking forward. Through the ages, nature has been linked to hope. When you take time to seek it and enjoy it, you may find that nature becomes an important part of your hope maintenance plan.

Family Interaction and Gatherings

Family milestones hold great significance. A wedding, a new grandchild, or a college graduation points to the future. Celebrating your own birthday (or that of your partner or child) or taking an anniversary trip all can help you feel hopeful. While it is good to be future oriented, it is equally important to draw happiness and hope from the present. Oftentimes, during periods of low hope, you might not feel like getting dressed, going out, and interacting with others. If you can possibly manage it, go. You never know where and when hope will be found.

At times, you may need to modify your hope. It may become necessary to refocus your hope kaleidoscope, to shift pieces and perspective. Despite this, you must never stop hoping. One excellent piece of advice is attributed to Greg Anderson, who wrote the book *Cancer Conqueror*: "Hope and hopelessness are both choices; always choose hope."

Preventing Hopelessness

Both the Bible and the Qur'an contain the story of Job and his suffering. In the Bible's version (Job 17:15), Job expresses his despair amid overwhelming misfortune, "And where is now my hope—Who can see any hope for me?"

When a person feels hopeless, he or she is no longer able to see a viable response to a threat. Hopelessness means an inability, even after repeated efforts, to bring about the desired or necessary change. It is feared that a dreaded outcome will occur and that nothing can stop it. As a result, a person becomes helpless; they feel trapped.

Despite these overwhelming feelings, hope still exists. As one long-time hope researcher, Alphonous Obayuwana, contends, "True hopelessness, or 'Zero Hope,' is unknown. It is simply unimaginable."

A hope crisis is often sudden—when hopes are dashed—but it can have a slower onset when one goal after another is missed or proven to be unattainable. Sometimes we use phrases like "I felt my hope slipping away" or "My hope started fading." One important thing about a crisis of hope is that it provides an opportunity for evaluating and, if necessary, resetting your goals or refocusing your hope.

Managing a Crisis of Hope

> After the usual biopsies and other tests, I was told that I had a potentially fatal disease. Now that gets your attention. The Big C. The word "cancer": it overwhelms the psyche—just the word. I couldn't believe it. I was unprepared for the enormous emotional jolt that I received from the diagnosis.
> —Sandra Day O'Connor, Associate Justice, US Supreme Court

We all have a definition for what we consider a crisis, for what level a situation and its accompanying stress must reach before we apply a crisis label. For most people, obvious examples of a life crisis are major events like being diagnosed with a serious illness, the death of a loved one, loss of a job, bankruptcy, or the end of a significant relationship. Then there are the smaller problems in living that may seem like a crisis—a car breaking down, storm damage to our home, or a legal issue. These may create high levels of stress, but they are not the same as a crisis. Often, stress—even cumulative stress—can be managed using usual coping methods. What might be harder to define is what constitutes a crisis of hope.

Despite our personal understandings of a crisis, there is an entire psychological theory built around the concept. The word *crisis* has its roots in a Greek word meaning "decision," or more broadly, "a turning point." A simple definition is that a "crisis is an upset in a steady state." During a crisis, an individual enters what is called a period of cognitive confusion. That means the person has no usual and adequate problem-solving skills for the situation, does not even know how to think about the problem or evaluate it or its possible outcomes, much less make a decision. A crisis is a period of uncertainty that may also be accompanied by fear, dread, panic, and anger. For a time, at least, the obstacle seems insurmountable. In short, the person is overwhelmed.

Crises tend to have certain typical phases—a beginning, middle, and end. At the same time, and perhaps a bit more on the positive side, a crisis generally is time limited. It usually lasts for one to six weeks. By then, either the crisis has resolved, the individual has found a way to deal with it on an ongoing basis, or the problem is avoided by a relinquishment or reestablishment of goals.

At the conclusion of a crisis, when a solution is found, things may return to normal, to the previous steady state. Or the crisis may be resolved, but the result is a lower level of functioning or lower level of mental health. Or the solution may lead to a more adequate or higher level of functioning.

When concerned about holding on to hope at a critical or difficult time, it may seem irrelevant or frivolous to speak about a crisis as an opportunity or to note that the Chinese characters that compose the word *crisis* mean "danger" and "opportunity." Yet many experts believe that a crisis can inspire new vision, encourage creative thinking, and result in clearer goals and better strategies to solve the problem at hand. During a hope crisis, this can mean assessing if you need to evaluate your hope goals or develop new hope strategies to maintain or increase your hope for the future.

It may take some time to move past a hope crisis, and at some points or critical junctures, you may—in fact, probably will—need to seek additional information and support. However, unlike some other crises, since you are the one who decides for what and how you hope, you actually hold the personal power and have the ability to determine, redefine, and manage your hope. The most important thing is that you never give up hope, and that you recognize that there is always something to hope for.

Resiliency and Hope

Resiliency means being able to bounce back. It is the ability to cope with repeated stress and successfully negotiate risk, even severe risk. It refers to the personal qualities and community resources needed to rebound from adversity, trauma, loss, threats, and other major stressors. Resilience includes self-protective behaviors and strengths that allow a person to live life with a sense of mastery, competence, and hope. Some theorists claim that resiliency begins as soon as a threat is detected. At that moment, a resilient individual begins to form goals and set strategies for carrying out the goals. In other words, the process of hoping begins.

Never underestimate your capacity for finding, maintaining, and when necessary, regaining hope. You may find it helpful to read stories of individuals who overcame problems and stressors similar to the ones you are facing. One such frequently recommended resource is the book *Hope Dies Last: Keeping the Faith in Troubled Times* by Studs Terkel. Do whatever is needed to be hope resilient. Ask for assistance, borrow hope, and be your own best advocate.

Self-Advocacy and Hope

To maintain hope and to meet your hope goals, self-advocacy is essential. At times of great stress and adversity, your capacity to be self-reliant and resourceful may appear to be temporarily diminished. You know that moving forward is necessary, but you may not know how to do so. Perhaps the most important thing you can do when faced with a hope crisis, a new setback, or a discouraging outcome is to take time to fully evaluate the situation. A key to effective self-advocacy is determining clear goals and a deliberate path for action.

There are several reasons for self-advocacy regarding hope. First is that your hope belongs to you. Only you truly understand it and its meaning and importance. Others may support your goals, but you and you alone are responsible for determining what you will hope for and how you will work to attain the future you envision.

Standing up for your hope is critical. Sometimes it may be necessary to distance yourself from negative people. If you cannot avoid them, you may have to be direct and tell a well-meaning family member, friend, or acquaintance that you need to be surrounded by people who are positive and who will help you maintain your hope. If they are able, ask them to join you in your vision of hope. If not, ask them to refrain from saying unhelpful things.

Always keep in mind that you have the right to be hopeful. It may be necessary to seek a second, even a third, opinion to fully grasp your options. This applies to many of life's major problems, whether health related, business related, family related, or finance related. Self-advocacy skills, like the skills needed for managing your hope, can be learned and strengthened. If necessary, you can become a better communicator, a better decision-maker, and a better negotiator.

Finally, self-advocacy can give you a sense of stability and some feeling of control. It can also mitigate feelings of powerlessness and helplessness and prevent you from moving into hopelessness.

If you ever feel you are in danger of becoming hopeless, professional intervention may be necessary. Do not hesitate to seek assistance or ask for help. A professional social worker, psychologist, nurse, or member of the clergy can help you reframe your hopes. If you are low on hope, they will support you, even lend you some of their hope, until your own hope level rebounds.

Hope Highlights

- Don't ever underestimate your capacity for hope.
- Hope is like a kaleidoscope with many pieces, and the picture changes as circumstances change.
- Self-advocacy is essential to hope.
- You have the right to be hopeful.

CHAPTER SIX

Helping a Loved One Sustain Hope

It is in the shelter of each other that the people live.
—Irish proverb

As mentioned previously, each of us learns to hope based on a particular set of factors, circumstances, and experiences. Families, too, think about and use hope differently. They have patterns or what are called family hope constellations or family hope structures.

Family Hope

Some families use a religious framework for their hope. They believe in and rely on their religious training and on their faith. They may find inspiration and guidance in readings from the Bible or other religious works, and they may find comfort in religious or spiritual ritual or symbolism, and in visiting their church, synagogue, or mosque. They may attend religious events, and participate in activities such as prayer circles. If they have a strong religious constellation, they often affirm their beliefs publicly.

This is the family who believes that their future and the current problem is in God's hands, and they enlist their spiritual beliefs for problem-solving and in the healing process. On occasion, this may conflict with science, technology, or medicine. Given the potential for success in a treatment protocol or clinical trial, for example, they may reject the stated odds, saying "Only God can know the outcome, so I don't care about the statistics."

If ill or hospitalized, someone using this hope framework may ask to be visited by pastoral care or their own religious leader or ask their doctor or nurses to join them in prayer before a surgical procedure. Whenever possible, the patient and family may defer decision-making until there has been time for spiritual reflection.

In contrast to the religious hope constellation is the family who is more focused on science. This family may make most decisions based on research, facts, and statistics. If there is a health concern, they may seek opinions from various experts, weighing the options and odds prior to making a treatment decision. While they may be members of a faith community, their hope is informed more by evidence than by spirituality. If the statistics are positive and there is a consensus among experts, they feel hopeful and more confident about moving forward. A patient from this family might welcome a research report about a new clinical trial or a suggestion of a well-known specialist. However, this individual or family may not feel comfortable about a visit from someone in the religious community, and prayer may not be a hope strategy for them. They are not looking for someone who is a "priest-physician," but are seeking the most talented and skillful clinicians they can find.

These examples are used to highlight how hope differs from family to family and from individual to individual. What we learn from our families forms the basic building block for our hope. Our formal education may add to that hope constellation, or we may decide to eliminate or reject some aspect of what our families believe and how they use hope.

Next come our life experiences and relationships. These will either reinforce or influence our understanding and our use of hope. Choosing a life partner may strengthen our established family hope pattern or further modify it. Your children will be influenced by your blended family hope, and theirs may differ at some point from that of either your own or your partner's family of origin.

Family Communication

Given the complexity of hope, how is it possible to help a loved one maintain hope? First and foremost, don't use the situation to try to impose your own vision of hope. Instead, ask them about how they use hope and what hope means to them. Ask how you can be helpful and how you can best support them. During a crisis, especially a crisis of hope, your loved one may be vulnerable. That is not the time to try and convince them of the need to adopt or return to a religion, or to enroll in that clinical trial you found online, or to make a business decision you think is best.

Don't ask a pastor or rabbi or other religious leader to come for a surprise visit with your loved one or put their name on a public prayer list without consulting with them first. While prayer may be helpful to you, it may prove awkward for your loved one, and a forced interaction may simply cause embarrassment or alienation. The same is true with an estranged family member or friend. An attempt at reconciliation, which might seem hopeful to you, may not be desirable and may require more energy from your loved one than what is available.

Similarly, do not make any appointments or decisions for them without their knowledge and consent. It is, after all, their life, and it is their hope that is at stake. Another thing to always keep in mind is that hope deserves a high level of confidentiality. If someone is willing to disclose their hopes and fears, you should recognize how personal and important and private these disclosures are, and you should treat the information with great discretion.

It is also not your role to protect a loved one from information they need to know for their decision-making, even if it is done with the intent of maintaining their hope. As so many experts have emphasized, hope is too important to be sacrificed to untruths or evasions. You may think that you are helping by withholding bad news or by slightly misguiding them, but you are not. Misguided hope has a way of backfiring. Instead, use this time to help your loved one reframe their hope and reset their hope goals.

In a similar fashion, if a loved one's situation has changed, and it requires a change in outlook and goal-directed behavior, refusing to acknowledge the necessity for change places an undue burden on the person most affected by the issue. When a person is trying to maintain hope in the face of personal threat, it is unfair to insist that they rise to the level of your hope or that they join in your denial.

Differences of opinion among family members about the severity of problems are not uncommon, and they can stand in the way of viable solutions. You can't just wish a problem away. If, for example, one person fears that a teenager is becoming "too thin" while another sees only the success of her dieting, little action will be taken until a crisis point is reached. Or an adult child worries that a parent's drinking is becoming a problem. The other parent dismisses the concern, saying it is simply a response to stress—until a traffic accident results in a summons for driving while intoxicated.

You may remember that childhood game called "pass it on." One person whispers a secret to another person, who tells the next person, and so on. By the time the message gets to the end of the line, it sounds quite different from what was originally said. The same outcome can occur with family communication. Each of us hears what is said differently. We use our own frame of reference, and we tend to filter out certain things—especially things we do not want to accept. When a worry turns into a crisis, though, denial no longer can be maintained. At that point, hope—realistic hope—with goals for achieving a desired outcome is needed. The following example shows how denial can affect family communication.

Case Example: Communication Clouded by Denial

A couple named Bill and Linda are struggling with a family crisis. Bill was diagnosed with a serious illness several months ago and is undergoing treatment. He just finished an appointment with his physician, who told him the treatment regimen did not appear to be working as well as they had hoped. He said they could continue it for another few weeks and then reevaluate, but the doctor thinks a different—more rigorous—therapy will be needed shortly. Bill is disappointed but not actually surprised. He has not been feeling very well. He went back to work a few weeks ago but has found it to be quite an effort. He is not sure he can continue on a full-time basis. Bill has not discussed this with Linda because she seems so happy that he is working again.

Bill tells Linda what the doctor told him, that his current treatment might not be working. Linda had been hoping for good news. She had been so relieved when Bill returned to work because it seemed like their family life was returning to normal. A different treatment might reverse all of the progress they have made getting their lives on track once again. As a result, Linda refuses to hear what Bill is trying to tell her—that he knows he isn't getting better, that he is sure the doctor is right. He would like to rethink their plans for the next few months. Linda insists things will be better by the time Bill next sees the doctor. She shuts down any talk of changing plans and tells Bill he must keep his hopes up. She tells him he needs to get to the gym more often and eat a healthier diet.

It is not unusual for family members to have divergent hopes, to be at different places on the hope continuum. In fact, people—even family members—do not have identical levels of hope, do not use the same hoping strategies, or do not reformulate hope at the same pace. As noted earlier, hope is individual, and even when faced with the same situation, people hope in their own way. Would Linda's response have been the same if she had been in the room during Bill's discussion with his physician? Perhaps. She would have heard the same conversation, rather than Bill's filter. She may have had the opportunity to ask a few clarifying questions, but she still may have been guarded against bad news and internalized the conversation in a more positive way.

Linda's being hopeful is not a bad thing, but she needs to guard against using her hope as a shield or a form of denial or against imposing her hopes on Bill. Her hope may help bolster Bill's lowered hope, but Bill's hope level and his perception are both valid and should not be discounted.

Bill does need to prepare for starting more rigorous therapy. He has looked at the research, and he has a realistic understanding of what the new treatment will entail. He may be correct that it is time for him to reframe his hope and set some more realistic goals. Since he is struggling with work demands now, he needs to discuss the possibility of cutting back on his hours or working from home some days. He and Linda need to review how they will manage financially and whether or not he should apply to use disability insurance. They also need to discuss what they will tell their children and family members.

There are many barriers to good family communication. Denial is only one of them. Others include fear, guilt, anger, inability to confront, refusal to discuss bad news or sad topics, and different coping styles. Without open and honest communication, dealing effectively with a family crisis, and maintaining family hope become almost unmanageable. The family as a unit may be at risk, further compounding the crisis at hand.

Family Burnout

It is extremely difficult to endure a loved one's powerlessness or witness their distress and suffering, whether physical, emotional, or existential. You may be frightened for them and frightened for yourself and your family. Sometimes, the challenge seems too daunting, too prolonged. Individual family members or the entire family may teeter on burnout.

Burnout is a term generally applied to individuals, especially those who do "people work," meaning they spend considerable time with others under conditions of chronic tension and stress. Burnout is a state of emotional exhaustion. Its signs and symptoms vary and cover the gamut from physical symptoms such as fatigue and minor illnesses, to psychological symptoms such as anger and depression, to behavioral outcomes such as avoidance, escapism, or harmful activities. Feelings of being unappreciated or feeling indispensable often accompany burnout. Members of a family may exhibit different individual symptoms, but when taken together, the family unit may be experiencing burnout.

Living with uncertainty and setbacks is exhausting. Families under great stress have a decreased ability to make decisions or solve problems. They recognize that moving forward is important, but they may not know how to do so. Individual family members may have difficulty maintaining their own level of hope, and they may have limited energy to support one another because all of their attention is focused on the situation at hand and on the loved one who is at the heart of the struggle. As a result, families can magnify a patient's hopelessness.

Often, a family crisis requires some change in family roles and responsibilities, in finances, and in usual ways of functioning. These changes should be discussed directly, and the loved one should be part of the family conversation and part of the decision-making whenever possible. Families also must guard against allowing one person to assume the bulk of the work or the worry or to become the rescuer or the family martyr. One of the clues to individual burnout is when a person begins to think they are indispensable. They feel they cannot take a break or a short vacation. They stop doing things for themselves like attending church or going to the gym or taking care of their own health and personal needs. At critical times, the family needs to seek as much outside assistance as they can, whether physical care for their loved one, professional advice, or personal support.

A family in crisis also must resist the urge to meet every challenge with the same energy. Some issues and decisions can be deferred until later. It is important to take time to evaluate a new situation and do some thinking about it and planning as a family. If one person is particularly good at planning, let them help organize things, including schedules and to-do lists and seeking resources as needed.

In times of family burnout, each family member, and the family as a whole, needs hope support. Without it, they may become hopeless together. This can be achieved by surrounding yourself with helpful people who generate hope. Attending an educational or support group can help. When necessary, find a hope expert—a family therapist, social worker, or other counselor—who can help you keep or revise your perspective, who can help enhance family communication, and who can help your family maintain hope.

As hard as it may be to keep your own hope active, your individual hope must actually remain secondary to the hope of your loved one who is struggling and is at the heart of the crisis. What is needed most is for you to be present, caring, and encouraging. This means respecting and supporting their vision of hope, not "trying to help them be more realistic" or diminishing their hope in any way. In fact, your most important goal is to protect your loved one from hopelessness. This means helping them remain open to possibilities, reminding them that there is always something to hope for, and encouraging them to choose hope no matter what the change in circumstances. While you are at it, make certain that you, too, always choose hope.

For many years Ellen Stovall was the leader of the National Coalition for Cancer Survivorship. A forty-five-year cancer survivor of several different cancers, Ellen strongly believed in hope. Her words emphasize the important linkage between communication and hope:

> With communication comes understanding and clarity; with understanding, fear diminishes; in the absence of fear, hope emerges; and in the presence of hope, anything is possible.

Hope Highlights

- Hope differs from family to family and person to person.
- Truth is essential for hope.
- It is difficult to witness a loved one's distress and suffering.
- Families, like individuals, can experience burnout and may require hope support.

CHAPTER SEVEN

Finding Hope at the End of Life

Hope never abandons you:
you abandon it.
—George Weinberg

Most people find it difficult to think about death. We try hard to keep thoughts of ourselves or our loved ones dying in the back of our minds, as something that will not happen for a very long time. In addition, America has been described as a death-avoiding society. Despite growth in hospice services and palliative care, few individuals are comfortable with thinking or talking about end-of-life issues.

On the other hand, we use death to sell movies, magazines, newspapers, and video games. We see actual and horrific acts of torture and killings streamed online, yet we do not know what to say when someone is diagnosed with a serious illness. We watch police dramas where, show after show, the phrase "sorry for your loss" is the quick phrase for expressing sympathy, yet few people know how to write notes of condolence after the death of a loved one or colleague.

This contradiction of flaunting death for publicity purposes on the one hand yet avoiding or hiding death in real life was labeled the "pornography of death" by British anthropologist Geoffrey Gorer. In short, death used this way is divorced from its natural emotion, which is grief. If even our society works against an acceptance of death, how can an individual envision and work toward a meaningful and peaceful end of life—his or her own death? How can a person remain positive? What can one even hope for at such a difficult and traumatic time?

As previously noted, hope is flexible, and it can change as situations change. It can be reframed, and the usual strategies for maintaining hope can be redrafted as required. But can hope really exist and be meaningful when a life-threatening condition exists, when an illness is rapidly progressing and there appears to be no way to stop or reverse its course?

Health-care professionals and experts on hope emphasize that not only is it possible to have hope at the end of one's life—it is essential. It is hope that makes the dying process tolerable. It is hope that allows a person to live fully until the moment of death. It is hope that encourages the review and integration of meaning over one's life course. It is hope that ensures quality of life during the final weeks and days, and it is hope that supports your family during their sadness and grief. It is hope that gives some assurance of competency when things seem to be flying out of control.

Elisabeth Kübler-Ross—a psychiatrist who, in the late 1960s and early 1970s, conducted one of the first groundbreaking studies about death and dying—emphasized that death is the final stage of personal growth. Granted, when a person is approaching the end of his or her life, time takes on new meaning and validity. It becomes more precious. As a result, it requires a sharp focus on the here and now, rather than thinking only about life fading away or dwelling on how much or little time is left.

This requires a change in your relationship to time. It necessitates a shift from what you were hoping for in the future to what you want to do and be during your remaining life span. It requires determining new and achievable goals so that you can live as fully as possible until you die. Even in extreme circumstances, there are choices to make and, perhaps, lessons to be learned.

So what are the possible hopes for end of life? First is that hope is linked to some sense of control, even if limited, both of oneself and over one's environment. We may not be able to know or predict the actual timing of our deaths, but most people know when it is approaching and getting closer. There are practical things you can do to help you find some measure of peace and to help your family when your death does occur. Completing an advance directive for end-of-life care and specifying what you request and prefer is really a caring gift for your family. As difficult as it may be to contemplate, letting your final wishes be known and having final plans in place are essential. Your family may resist these conversations. They may say they do not want to discuss such negatives or admonish you to keep your hopes up—to stop thinking that way—but there is probably little that is more important than completing this legal document. Other important legal issues such as completing a will, transferring ownership of some assets and possessions, and discussing funeral arrangements will be an immense help to your loved ones after your death.

In addition to a general will, some individuals find it desirable to compose what is referred to as an ethical will. Originally, ethical wills were ancient documents used in the Judeo-Christian tradition in medieval times. The purpose was to pass ethical or spiritual values from one generation to another, usually from a father to his children. Perhaps just as importantly, the ethical will linked the writer with both their history and the future. Today ethical wills may be referred to as legacy letters or life legacy letters. These differ from regular wills in that they are usually shared with the intended recipients prior to death. If the recipients are too young (or perhaps not even born yet), an ethical will can be especially meaningful later on for helping children or grandchildren understand the history of family values and what you personally valued during your life. There are excellent written and online resources available for completing such a document.

You may have specific questions about the dying process itself and about the actual moment of death. Your physician or a hospice nurse can provide honest and caring answers. You will have to determine if you wish to die at home and who will care for you. Who would you like to be present? What will happen to your body at the time of death and afterward? Can they assure you that any pain or suffering can and will be alleviated?

Just reading the above paragraph may have made you anxious and sad. Try to keep in mind that you need information so you and your loved ones can be as prepared as possible. Once you have these critical decisions made, you can move forward with other aspects of your life.

In addition to controlling the details of your dying, what other hopes are viable? If we return to the types of hope—generalized, particularized, and transcendent—different goals for each type of hope can emerge.

Examples of generalized hopes may be that, as much as possible, you maintain your dignity or your sense of humor, and that despite any disability or frailty, others continue to recognize the essential "you" and treat you the same way they always have. You may hope to make your love of family and friends clear, and you may hope to demonstrate a calmness and acceptance that will assist your loved ones during their grieving process. Your hopes may include achieving the best quality of life possible and living as fully as you can each day—what has been termed "living your dying."

Your own particular hopes will depend on what is and has been important in your life. One person may hope to finish documenting a family history, while another may hope to have the time and energy to write letters to each of their children or siblings and tell them what they have meant to their lives. Many people wish to visit a family home or a special vacation spot once again. Others hope to be able to restate wedding vows on a certain date or celebrate an anniversary in a special way. There are also life events that individuals hope to live long enough, and be healthy enough, to be able to attend—a college graduation, a birth, or a party for the return of a family member who was serving in the military in another country.

It may be of great importance and a particular hope to be able to disburse of some special possessions, such as giving an engagement ring or other special jewelry to a daughter or a wristwatch to a son or asking your sister to accept some family or personal artwork. If a writer or an artist, a person may hope to donate their collection to a university or gallery and live long enough to be able to attend the dedication.

Then there are the smaller, everyday happenings and pleasures that are meaningful and that contribute to the fullness of daily life. Many people hope to prolong and experience these as often as possible in whatever time remains. Having your morning coffee sitting on your deck, or lying beside your spouse and sleeping in your own bed at night are examples of such hopes.

Some people hope to make amends or apologize to a friend or relative they have offended or been alienated from for many years. Sometimes these reconciliations are possible; other times, they must remain unresolved. Perhaps the anger and hurt are too great, or the person's energy level simply is not adequate to meet the challenge, or there simply is not enough time.

The final category, transcendent hope, is often a search for meaning, for reviewing and accepting that life has meant something, that there have been personal accomplishments and achievements and satisfying relationships. In the psychological literature, this is referred to as a life review. It frequently involves another individual who is interested in your life story and offers you the opportunity to tell it. Life reviews are not generally about the history of one's religious life, (including confession or asking for forgiveness or atonement) even though the importance of religion or spirituality can be included. The story of Mr. J below is an example of such a review.

Case Example of Life Review

Mr. J was a business executive at a large corporation. He was admitted to the hospital after colon cancer spread to his liver. He was housed in the patient suite that was reserved by his company. There was no further treatment available for his cancer, so the goal was palliative care or symptom control.

Mr. J was a realist. He knew the facts and understood that he had a low probability for surviving for more than a few weeks. He had been married almost forty years and seemed very caring about his wife, Mary Jane.

The oncology social worker asked Mr. J to tell her a bit about his life. He began by describing a fairly happy childhood but also discussed a strained relationship with his father. The social worker and Mr. J fell into a routine. Each day that the social worker visited him, Mr. J would pick up where he left off in his narrative, sometimes saying. "Let's see, where were we yesterday?"

He divided his life story into decades. He discussed college, his marriage, his sequence of important business positions, and what he had done for his employees and his community.

Occasionally, Mr. J would remark that he hadn't thought about some event or relationship for a long time. He discussed his regrets as well as his successes. He was saddened that he and his wife had been unable to have a child or that he never did reconcile with his father, and he wished he had traveled more for pleasure. At no time during his recitation did he mention the seriousness of his condition or the fact that his life story was coming to an end. He seemed comfortable, both physically and emotionally.

After two weeks, Mr. J had reached the present time in his story. He said to the social worker, "And that's the sum total of my life." She remarked on how full and well-lived it had been, and Mr. J concurred. He then told the social worker that there was one more thing he wished to discuss. He said, "I want to talk about this only once and then not mention it again." He told her that he knew he wasn't going to survive his cancer and he had made his peace with that fact. However, he didn't think his wife was at the same place. He was worried she would have a difficult time after his death, and he asked if the social worker would be in touch with Mary Jane a few times to help her the way she had helped him.

Mr. J had been engaged in life review, a process of making meaning of his life. The social worker provided a nonjudgmental opportunity—a safe place—for Mr. J to discuss successes and failures, regrets and joys, strengths and vulnerabilities. In the end, he concluded that he had lived a full, good life, and he expressed a hope for the future—that his wife would be able to manage without him and that the social worker would help her.

While religion was not covered in Mr. J's life review, transcendent hope frequently does involve one's religious hopes or spiritual beliefs. It may entail prayer, ritual, or spiritual healing. It may mean facing and resolving spiritual pain, requiring the intercession of a member of the clergy, or it may involve individual sacredness, personal meditation, or private devotion.

Transcendent hope can stress the importance of having a strong faith, which can become an antidote to fear and anxiety. It may help a dying person reach acceptance and peacefulness. Rabbi Hirschel Jaffe, author of *Why Me? Why Not Me?* is also a four-time cancer survivor. When he was dealing with his own life-threatening illness, he proclaimed,

"We can find meaning and hope even in our darkest days." He also encouraged others to "live with your illness instead of considering yourself as dying from it."

Psychiatrist Avery Weisman, in his study of terminality, determined that "hope and acceptance of death are natural accompaniments of each other." Furthermore, Weisman found that "hope seems to have a way of outlasting illness." In a similar conclusion, psychologist Richard Boerstler and his coauthor Hulen Kornfeld noted, "The only requirement hope makes is that it be allowed to exist."

These sentiments are similar to an old Spanish proverb: *la esperanza muere al utimo*—hope dies last. This saying reemphasizes that there is always something to hope for and you should always, always choose hope.

Hope Highlights

- Hope is essential at end of life.
- Hope allows a person to live fully in whatever time they have.
- Hope and acceptance can exist together.
- Death is the final stage of personal growth.

CHAPTER EIGHT

Reclaiming Hope
after Grief

In the depth of winter, I finally learned
that within me there lay an invincible summer.
—Albert Camus

ost frequently, when we use the word *grief,* we
are referring to the death of a loved one. Grief,
though, can be much broader than that. Grief is
the normal reaction to any loss, whether the loss is personal,
interpersonal, material, or symbolic. For example, think
about the loss of a home due to a storm or fire, the loss of a
job, the loss of mobility, the loss of an important object like
a piece of meaningful jewelry, or temporary hair loss due to
chemotherapy. On the other hand, bereavement is a special
type of grief related to death. It includes intense mourning,
and it is experienced within social and cultural contexts.

Grief is as difficult to define as hope, and for the same
reasons. It is highly varied, individual, and complex, and is
affected by a variety of factors: individual strengths, depth

and meaning of the relationship to the deceased, type and timing of death, age of the griever, previous grief experience, cultural and social factors, and available support system. The list could go on. There is, however, general agreement about acute grief—what is referred to as "the symptomatology of acute grief."

Acute Grief

There may be differences depending on whether or not the death was expected and the intensity of the relationship to the individual who has died, but most frequently, acute grief includes some time (usually one to two weeks) when newly bereaved persons experience shock or numbness, when they can't quite grasp what is happening, or the reality or finality of the loss. They may need help with decisions and everyday tasks as simple as deciding what to wear and when to eat.

The numbness period includes and is almost always followed by what is referred to as waves of grief, generally lasting for thirty to sixty minutes at a time. These are expressions of intense emotional and bodily distress, including crying and sobbing, a feeling of tightness in the throat, a choking feeling with shortness of breath, an empty feeling in the abdomen, a lack of muscular power, and an excessive need for sighing. These waves are often accompanied by sadness, depression, restlessness, and the inability to sleep.

Grief also may include what is referred to as searching behavior—looking for the loved one, or thinking they see the loved one's face on a bus, or seeing the loved one walking down the street, or feeling certain their car has just pulled into the garage at the usual time. These are the result of certain visual and auditory cues that play into the feeling that a loved one cannot really be gone. Instead, they expect them to come walking through the door at any moment. This part of grief often frightens both the individual and the family members who have little experience with grief. Individuals fear they are going crazy, because they think they are having hallucinations. They are not. It is a normal part of grief, and these behaviors should not cause alarm.

A second aspect of grief that sometimes worries others is the use of linking objects. Wearing a piece of clothing or jewelry or sleeping with an item that belonged to the loved one makes the bereaved feel closer to the person who has died. This often provides great comfort and can be helpful for the bereaved. Understanding the elements of acute grief goes a long way to normalize the experience.

Living with Grief

In the past, there was a tendency to divide grief into stages and then encourage individuals to do the necessary grief work to move through each stage to resolve grief, to reach acceptance, to "get over it." This is similar to our society's approach to death—we try our best to deny it, keep it hidden if we can, and not make others uncomfortable. Added to this is the fact that most companies have inadequate leave for the death of a loved one. Many businesses limit bereavement leave to one to five days, depending on the relationship to the person who has died. Death of a spouse or child receives the maximum; grief for a grandparent or sibling may be allotted less time.

This diminution of grief goes hand in hand with the elimination of some rituals from the past that had been helpful to the grieving person and family. Viewings, wakes, and funerals have changed. More families are choosing cremation with a scattering of the ashes instead of burial, and memorial services and celebrations of life have replaced religious services that often included healing rituals. Short condolence messages are now easily sent electronically, and they lack a personal touch. Friends may wish to be supportive; they simply do not know how.

How can you learn to live with your grief and pain? How can you move forward? How can you find hope again? What do you have to be hopeful about—your loved one is gone! Will you ever feel joyful and happy once more?

Be Gentle and Kind to Yourself

First of all, begin by being gentle with yourself. Don't expect to rebound quickly or berate yourself for bad days. Recognize that grief is not linear. It is a winding path that requires adaptation and even, sometimes, a change of course. There may also be surprises waiting at some of the unexpected places or hidden turns. Nor does grief begin at a low point and then reach a high point (back to normal, for example) in a certain amount of time. Grief is known for its ups and downs. There are many anniversary reactions—birthdays, holidays, wedding anniversaries, and the anniversary of the date of the death. There are family events and other activities that you will need to attend for the first time without your loved one. Also, your memories of your loved one are intertwined with daily living—favorite places, restaurants, books, movies, and routines that can cause a temporary spike in your sadness.

While saying, "It will get better with time," seems too easy and too pat, time actually does help somewhat with anniversary reactions. You only have to go through each first anniversary without your loved one once.

If possible, try to plan for anniversary days. It might be useful to take a vacation day from work on an important date or plan some other event. Wear a meaningful piece of jewelry or prepare a special meal. Be with your grief on those days and acknowledge your sadness. Then move forward as best you can the following day.

Even with planning, you may find that smaller but no less painful episodes of acute grief occur for a long time. These may happen suddenly, seemingly without warning. Perhaps you hear a familiar song, smell a scent that your loved one wore, or simply have a thought or memory, and your grief comes rushing back. When this happens, remind yourself that the mini-episode of grief will pass, and you can return to your previous activity.

Tell Your Grief

In the play *Macbeth*, Shakespeare wrote, "Give sorrow words; the grief that does not speak knits up the o-er wrought heart and bids it break." We now recognize that talking about a loss—telling your grief story—is especially helpful, even necessary, for healing. The problem is that most people are unfamiliar with grief, and they do not know how to handle it or participate in it.

Today it is not unusual to get to middle age without experiencing the death of a loved one. As a result, we are uncomfortable responding to someone else's loss. This may include avoiding the person who is bereaved or at least avoiding any topics related to the death. Even close friends and family members discourage conversations about the person who has died or the loss in general. They frequently do this because they do not want to make the bereaved sad by talking about it. Many times, though, it is because they are personally uncomfortable with grief.

What we do know is that telling the loss story and talking about the loved one who has died is important, even critical. Repeated tellings help to make the loss real and help the bereaved resolve some doubts and, perhaps, find some meaning in the painful experience.

Case Example: Giving Expression to Grief

One grief researcher was conducting a study of older widows. The sample was women over seventy who had lost their spouses at least one year previously. It was not unusual for the women being interviewed to "begin at the beginning," saying something like, "I can clearly remember that first day he wasn't feeling well," or, "I remember exactly what I was doing when the police officer came to the door," or "I felt frightened when the phone rang." Many of the women had prepared for the interviews by getting out the obituary notice that was in the paper or the bereavement card from the burial service. Some had collected pictures and other special mementos. The interview provided an opportunity for a modified life review—a grief review. What was most poignant about these exchanges was how often the women told the researcher that they had not talked about the death since the funeral. When asked why, their replies were quite similar—that no one wanted to talk about it. Their children and grandchildren would discourage the conversations saying it would only make them sad. This meant the women often had no sanctioned outlets for their grief. They lacked needed support and felt like they were totally on their own

with their grief. As a result, they had to
hide their feelings and their sadness.

Contrast this case example to the Jewish customs for acknowledging, supporting, and recognizing grief, what is referred to as "sitting shivah." *Shivah*, from the Hebrew word meaning "seven," begins after the funeral and is a weeklong period of mourning where family members traditionally gather in the mourner's home to receive visitors and participate in traditional rituals like continuously burning a mourning candle and covering mirrors to evoke a period of self-reflection.

The mourners do not work or participate in outside events during shivah. The distinguishing factor is that mourners are completely separated from everyday life so they can focus exclusively on their grief and on the memory of their loved one. Visitors sit with the mourners and offer prayers and consolation. Shivah ends on the seventh day when the mourners rise from their mourning and return to normal routines. Some mourning practices, like avoiding entertaining events, are observed for another thirty days, and some practices are observed for the first year. These rituals provide both a way to honor the deceased and sanction an open expression of grief.

When someone tells you not to talk about your grief "because it upsets you or makes you sad," reply that it helps you to talk about it. If you have trouble finding someone who is comfortable listening, be proactive in seeking an outlet. Meet with your clergy, set up a meeting with a counselor, or attend a support group.

Find Support

Finding a support community after the death of a loved one can be especially helpful. A support group can provide the space and the permission to talk about your loss and your feelings. Many people find, however, that they are not immediately ready for a support group. They need a bit of time to get beyond acute grief or to regain the energy needed for attendance.

Hospices offer outstanding bereavement care, as do many hospital programs and some community agencies. Keep in mind that while there are some fairly universal reactions around grief, there are many different and subjective ones too. A support group for parents who have lost a child will differ from a group trying to deal with the loss of a spouse. Similarly, a group of individuals trying to move forward after the death of a loved one who committed suicide will differ from a group trying to survive the loss of a young adult to a drug overdose. Likewise, a young widows' group may differ from a group of older widows. Younger widows may be trying to manage children, a work schedule, and reengage socially. A group of women retirement age or older may have different concerns. They may be struggling more with loneliness, maintaining their homes, and their own health issues.

Sometimes a less formal group can help. In one very rural community, there were numerous older women who had been widowed and who supported one another. When a woman lost her husband, the group attended the viewing and funeral, and immediately began aiding the newly bereaved. In some ways, it was almost like the initiation into a club or sorority. The group provided advice, assistance like carpooling to the grocery store or church, and most important of all, an opportunity to discuss their loss and feelings. The newly widowed woman quickly realizes that she will not be alone and that she has others to help her with her grief.

Reframe the Content of Your Grief Story as Necessary

Self-talk, mentioned in the maintaining hope section, is the story you tell yourself about your loss and grief, and it can help you move forward or can keep you trapped in your sorrow. In her poem "Lament," written about grief, Edna St. Vincent Millay ends with, "Life must go on; I forget why." Statements like "I can't get through this," or, "I'll never be happy again" can be a self-fulfilling prophecy. After the death of a loved one, a readjustment is required in our way of looking at the world. We also must redefine our plans for living in it.

When you hear yourself sending negative messages, try your best to change that internal conversation. This is especially true with "should have" messages: I should have realized how sick he was; I should have done more, or cared more, or been more. Berating or blaming yourself only intensifies your grief. The following case example involves a woman who felt responsible for her husband's death.

Case Example: A Love Story of Loss

Pearl and Anthony had been happily married for sixty-two years. They had no children and were best friends as well as spouses. Anthony had heart disease but was doing fairly well until one weekend in late March. His ankles became swollen, and his breathing seemed a bit uneven. They hated to bother their longtime family doctor on the weekend, but Pearl was worried. She finally called him late Saturday afternoon. The doctor suggested a slight change to Anthony's medication and said he would see him Monday morning. Anthony continued to get worse. Very early Monday morning, Pearl called a taxi and took Anthony to the emergency room.

After several hours, Anthony's doctor came out to the waiting area to give Pearl the bad news that Anthony's heart had been overstressed, and that it had simply stopped working. He also added that Pearl should not have left the situation go so long. She should have gotten Anthony to the hospital sooner.

Pearl was devastated, not only by Anthony's death, but by her failure to help him in time. Months passed, and Pearl moved through the days almost in a fog. She neglected her appearance, stopped going out, and had only minimal contact with friends and others.

On December 24, Pearl was having a particularly hard time. It would be her first Christmas without Anthony in over six decades. Friends were urging her to attend Christmas Eve services, but she just didn't think she could manage it.

Late in the afternoon, the doorbell rang. There stood a delivery man with a box of flowers. A letter was taped to the box, and Pearl instantly recognized Anthony's handwriting. Pearl opened the envelope and started reading. It began, "My dearest Pearly, I couldn't stand the thought of you going through a Christmas without a present from me." Anthony had ordered the flowers and left the letter and instructions for a Christmas Eve delivery a few weeks before he died in March.

Pearl said that was a turning point in her grief. She realized that Anthony was still with her, that he was watching over her and waiting for her, and that he didn't blame her for his death. She did attend the evening's church service, and Anthony's gift and letter helped her move forward in her life.

There are several important points in this beautiful story of love. One is that our words have a power, and we should choose them carefully, especially when individuals are in a vulnerable position like Pearl was at the hospital. Second is that death ends a life; it changes, but does not end, the relationship. Pearl was still Anthony's wife. The letter reinforced that fact, and Pearl was certain she and Anthony would be reunited one day. Finally, no matter how forlorn a situation seems, hope after grief is possible and essential.

Just as people see symbols of hope in everyday and spiritual life, so, too, do many individuals perceive messages from their loved ones who have died. They may not be as direct as Pearl's letter above, but they can be meaningful and comforting. These are often described as coincidences—finding that special piece of jewelry on the anniversary of the day he gave it to you, or seeing her favorite hopeful poem when you are feeling low. One young woman described carrying on a daily conversation with her husband who had died suddenly. Others have related receiving messages from their loved ones in dreams.

Many people report that they would like to find linkages to, and receive messages from, their loved ones, but none are forthcoming. This adds to their feelings of loss and grief, even abandonment. To recognize such messages, you may need to be more open to the possibility, and sometimes even suspend your usual patterns of thinking.

Finding your own place and space for grieving is important. A grief sanctuary can allow you some time just "to be" rather than "to do." It may also help you find some peace and provide opportunity for rekindling your hope. Sitting in silence for a short period each day or meditating may help you regain perspective.

Bibliotherapy—using books, writings, and poems about the loss and grief of others—can also be an effective grief intervention. By reading about the experiences of others who have suffered loss, you may find some insight into your own grief. Creative arts are another way to express your grief. One community center offered a mask-making group, where persons struggling with grief could make masks and then discuss what their masks represented regarding their grief and feelings.

Get Help When Needed

It is possible to fall into, and get stuck in, the depths of grief. Acute grief causes a crisis for almost everyone, but like other crises, it should slowly flatten out, and intensity should begin to lessen as weeks go by.

One mother described what her grief felt like after the loss of her child to leukemia. She said that, at first, her grief was like total body pain. Every fiber of her body hurt. Then, one day the pain was just a bit less. Over the months, the pain continued to recede little by little. Eventually, the pain was contained in a special compartment in her heart. She said it was never not there and that at any given moment, she could reach back and feel it at full force, but it was now manageable, and she felt able to regain some control of her life once again.

Individuals don't "get over" their grief. Grief doesn't just "fade away." It doesn't get "finished," "resolved," or "worked through." The loss of a loved one is a part of our life, and like other life experiences, our grief becomes an integral part of our being. Grief can be debilitating and overwhelming, and we can live in a state of chronic grief, keeping grief at the forefront because the past seems a greater source of comfort than the future. Or we can learn from it, grow from it, and use what we have learned to help others, to be stronger and more compassionate. This is the hopeful side of grief—that some good may result, not from the loss of our loved one, but from what we do after that loss, how we use our grief, how we become stronger. Recovery from grief requires that we find renewed meaning in our life. We learn to hope and live again.

Just as hope changes as situations and circumstances change, your grief will change over time, but change requires courage. When first confronted by grief, you may have felt as broken as a big oak tree that had been shattered by wind and lightning. Like that tree, it is not possible to put your life back together in its exact previous form, but like an acorn buried at the roots of that broken tree, it is possible to start anew, to grow after a devastating loss.

Even when grief overwhelms your life, hope is there waiting. It hasn't been lost or destroyed. Hope will outlast your grief, and your hopes for the future will return. With hope, you will find peace and happiness once again. Always choose hope.

Hope Highlights

- Death ends a life, not a relationship.
- Grief must be expressed in some way.
- Personal growth sometimes follows grief.
- Hope will outlast grief.

CHAPTER NINE

Restoring Professional Hope

Although the world is full of suffering,
it is full also of the overcoming of it.
—Helen Keller

By and large, helping professionals tend to be hopeful and positive. They generally are dedicated, tenacious, and solution oriented. They have within themselves a reserve, a personal resiliency, which serves them well. They don't give up on others or situations easily. There are many challenging and emotional situations, however, where professional hope is tested time and again in daily work. For example:

- A nurse sitting throughout the night with four teenagers keeping a death watch for their mother.
- A social worker supporting a family whose three sons died of the same disease during one summer.

- A chaplain encouraging a mother to maintain her faith when her two children are struggling with advanced cystic fibrosis at the same time.
- A surgeon listening to a twelve-year-old diagnosed with sarcoma, who has already lost her arm and shoulder, trying to console her parents about her advancing disease.
- A genetic counselor explaining to a couple that the child they are expecting has a severe genetic abnormality.
- A commanding officer accompanying a family to welcome home a returning service member who has suffered traumatic injuries.
- A police officer informing a loved one that their child has died from an overdose.
- A psychologist counseling a family attempting to understand why a loved one committed suicide.
- A firefighter consoling a family who has lost all of their possessions in a major fire.
- A teacher reporting to authorities that she believes a student is being physically abused after noticing burns on his body.
- A nursing home administrator helping a family understand that their loved one must be transferred to a secure unit due to progressing dementia.
- A psychiatrist confirming a diagnosis of schizophrenia for a young adult.

Examples like these are not uncommon, and you could easily add to the list and to the types of professionals and volunteers who struggle with difficult and hope-draining experiences on a fairly regular basis. Other people may discount the personal impact of these experiences by assuming that professionals get used to it or by reminding them that they chose their field. What did they expect?

It is nowhere near that simple. Certainly, first responders and helping professionals are trained in distance compassion, in guarding against transference, in using rigorous self-care, and in maintaining their emotional balance. Those are the first lines of defense for avoiding burnout and maintaining hope. Sometimes, however, both hope and professional stamina run low, and hope support is required.

Witnessing suffering is hard. Witnessing suffering on a regular basis tends to leave an emotional legacy, and it changes individuals in both profound and subtle ways. Few people think about the toll this takes on the professional helper who cannot avoid being affected by the suffering, loss, grief, and helplessness experienced by those they are trying to serve. They themselves may experience feelings of loss and professional grief, a grief that is not acknowledged or sanctioned. This is what Kenneth Doka has described as disenfranchised grief, when society does not recognize one's need, right, role, or capacity to grieve. Therefore, feelings must be hidden; there is no acceptable outlet for them. Grief, like stress, can accumulate. Eventually, a helping professional can face burnout.

The concept of burnout was developed in the early 1970s and is defined as a depletion of energy, a syndrome of emotional exhaustion and depersonalization experienced by individuals who feel temporarily overwhelmed by the problems of others. The phrase used in current literature to describe this syndrome is *compassion fatigue*. Professionals who work in high-stress and high-loss environments are more susceptible to it.

Usually, burnout is a gradual process, and it is almost always reversible. The best thing one can do is to be alert to symptoms that indicate they may be struggling and may need some assistance. These include physical symptoms like headaches, frequent colds, fatigue, exhaustion, or sleeplessness; emotional or psychological symptoms such as cynicism, anger, depression, guilt, detachment, or feelings of helplessness; or behavioral symptoms such as feeling unable to adequately meet the demands of their job, or by working longer hours, or by feeling indispensable. Underlying all of these symptoms may be a loss of professional hope.

Periodic feelings of hopelessness and helplessness are common. The surgeon may curse the slowness of finding a cure for pediatric cancer. The police officer may be angry that our country is not more focused on drug abuse. The military attaché may hate the war.

These, however, may be offset by a sense of accomplishment one experiences in helping others cope with adversity. For example, the nurse mentioned above received letters for a decade from the teenage daughter who lost her mother that night. The young man with schizophrenia responded to treatment. The injured veteran had intensive rehabilitation, and his family did well again. Through education and counseling, the family of the person who committed suicide learned that they were not to blame and that there was nothing they could have done to prevent the death.

Most professionals do not enter their fields equipped to deal with suffering. They are unprepared for multiple losses, professional grief, and bereavement overload. They spend years developing a balance of compassion and involvement, trying to emotionally protect themselves while supporting and helping others during times of great difficulty. To be successful, they must find ways to maintain professional hope.

Case Example: Professional Hope

A group of friends had gathered for Bonnie's celebration. She was retiring after spending twenty-five years working on a pediatric oncology unit at a medical center. One person noted how relieved Bonnie must be to finally be finished with such a sad job—working with sick children, many of whom had died. Another asked how Bonnie had managed to stay for so long. Still another noted that Bonnie must have been depressed much of the time. How was it possible to remain hopeful over the years?

Bonnie replied that her friends had it all wrong, that she had loved working there. In fact, she said it was one of the best jobs in the world, and she had been honored to be among such children. She related that the children she worked with were strong and courageous. From them she learned about honesty, humor, and true hopefulness. She said they taught her about the goodness of the human spirit and the meaning of love.

She said she wished other professionals could have such a remarkable experience and could leave their jobs knowing, with certainty, that they had made a difference. Yes, she was sad when a child lost his or her battle or when she witnessed the grief of parents and siblings. She had to keep in mind that, even though short, this was each child's life. They had lived fully and in the moment in whatever time they were given. She concluded that there were many lessons to be learned from seriously ill children, but one of the most important was that there was always a reason for hope.

C. Murray Parkes, one of the world's foremost experts on grief, emphasizes what Bonnie had discovered during her twenty-five years, that professionals can overcome the sadness they experience and can even grow from it. Parkes stated, "With proper training and support, we shall find that repeated griefs, far from undermining our humanity and our care, enable us to cope more confidently and more sensitively with each succeeding loss."

There are many personal strategies that can help you prevent or reverse burnout and remain engaged and hopeful. A few of these include the following:

- Knowing your own strengths and weaknesses, both personally and professionally.
- Being attentive to yourself and seeking support and assistance when needed.
- Keeping a balance between the personal, professional, and spiritual aspects of your life.
- Seeking expert clinical supervision.
- Continuing professional education.
- Building and maintaining a personal support system outside of your work environment.
- Joining a peer support network.
- Engaging in rigorous self-care.
- Sharing the emotional burden and stress of your job with coworkers.
- Reevaluating measures of success to include more than therapeutic outcomes.
- Setting aside time to deal with your feelings and concerns.
- Understanding your own definition of hope and the strategies you use to maintain it.
- Being open to hope wherever it is found.
- Keeping a journal of hope and psychosocial successes.

Professionals who regularly work with individuals facing the end of their lives, or who work in high-loss environments, need to find meaning in their clinical exchanges and in the comfort and support they provide to others. Their jobs are challenging, but as Bonnie mentioned above, there is the opportunity for success in each professional encounter. Professionals should never overlook, or discount, the importance of helping an individual or family find or maintain hope for living despite dying, or helping a person die well, or helping a family move forward with their own lives after the death of a loved one. Each of these successes requires the presence and utilization of hope. There is always enough hope to meet the needs. As poet Ralph Waldo Emerson so beautifully admonishes us, "The new day is too dear, with its hopes and invitations, to waste a moment of it." Always choose hope.

Hope Highlights

- Most helping professionals are resilient.
- Witnessing suffering changes a person.
- Professional grief is unsanctioned, but it is manageable.
- Burnout may occur, but it is usually temporary and reversible.

CHAPTER TEN

Building Communities of Hope

It is impossible to find sufficient hope just in ourselves.
—Jonathan Baptist Metz

There are many ways to define a community, and there are different characteristics to describe each. Probably the first thing the word brings to mind is a community of place—where you are from or where you live.

Then there is the use of the word *community*, meaning "an organized network with a common agenda," what might be called a community of interest. Examples would include the faith community or the business community.

There are communities of action (political action committees, advocacy groups), communities of practice (the medical community, the online community), and communities of circumstance (military families, college community). We have community centers and community agencies, community service, community networks, and community organizers. We speak of community spirit, community pride, and community celebrations.

While the above designations sound positive, not all communities serve a positive purpose. Based on some perceived negative characteristic, there have been times when the concept of community has been used for exclusion. The term *AIDS community* of the 1980s comes immediately to mind; the term led to stigma, discrimination, and blame.

The root of the word *community* comes from the Latin word *communitas*, meaning "shared in common." It is also the basis for the words *common* and *communication*. Generally, we see it as a positive to be a part of a group or network. We teach teamwork in our schools and sports, and we reward group efforts in the workplace. What makes communities so desirable? It could be identity, commonality, purpose, support, belongingness, or a sense of inclusion. All of these are important, but perhaps none is more important than a community that provides hope.

Sometimes when no formal community exists, people create one. The following description of a "community of crisis" is an example of an informal community joining together for the purpose of hope development and hope maintenance.

Case Example: A Crisis Community of Hope

The place is a waiting room area of a hospital intensive care unit that serves a large rural area. At any given time, there are usually eight or ten patients in the unit. The waiting area is always fairly crowded. Most of the patients live a distance away so family members don't go back and forth more than once a day. Many families stay at the two motels nearby.

Several patients have been in the unit for an extended period of several weeks. It is a small space, and there is no way to easily avoid one another. It also has a rural feel, and most people are friendly and polite. An informal division of labor has evolved. One person brings in doughnuts in the morning. Another helps with coffee. One acclimates family members who are new to the experience, discussing hospital practices and procedures. Still another is the expert on community resources—the best places to stay or eat, or how to get a closer parking space.

Most importantly, though, this crisis community provides support and hope. All of the different family members have a common purpose—waiting for their loved ones to get well enough, to pull through the medical crisis, so they can leave the unit and go home. They seem to recognize the importance of hope in such a desperate situation,

and they have become hope provid-
ers for one another. The word *hope* is
heard frequently: "I hope he has a good
night tonight," "I hope you can get
some rest," or "I hope things get better tomorrow." The word *prayer* also is
intermingled—"I'll say a prayer that his
procedure goes well" or "I'll keep your
family in my prayers tonight." Even if
the person who is the recipient of the
comments is not religious or spiritual,
the words themselves sound caring and
comforting.

While a new person may begin her
or his tenure at the unit desiring privacy
or trying to avoid entering into conversations, it is difficult to remain an out-
sider when people seem so well-meaning. There is a feeling of shared crisis
and a feeling of communal hope.

When our own personal hope gets low, we need assistance. Hope is not just a personal resource. Hope is best
when it is something we do together, when the community
also assumes responsibility for providing hope.

There are many excellent examples of community agencies that have hope as part of their mandate. The Boys and
Girls Club of America, the Cancer Support Community,
local thrift shops, and religious and veterans groups provide
hope along with needed services. The book *Hope Matters:*

The Power of Social Work provides numerous narratives of how hope can be a factor at all levels—for personal growth, in the community, and in society.

Probably nowhere are communities of hope more needed than in our current health-care centers and treatment programs. Health and mental health services have become almost proscriptive and highly regulated by insurance companies and government agencies. Health-care practitioners now operate under strict guidelines that often determine how long a patient can be admitted to a facility or program, how long they can receive therapies, and what drugs can be prescribed. For example, Medicare determines the amount of time a person can be covered by the hospice insurance benefit.

Cost cutting has also resulted in institutions and agencies eliminating many support services that used to be available for individuals and their families. Education programs, nutrition and other types of counseling, support groups, and bereavement follow-up are examples of assistance and positive support that used to be fairly routine. These were some of the "extras" that often helped those in a health-care crisis find a needed support system, and become part of a community of hope.

As a result, changes are now required to fill some of the gaps. We need our programs and facilities to infuse patient-centered care with hope-centered care. By doing so, communities of hope can be established and maintained. Communities of hope in health care have several essential characteristics. They foster trust and openness. They provide support and continuity of care, and they use a holistic and strengths-based approach.

These programmatic changes will require making enough time for interaction and explanation, and viewing the patient and family not only as the unit of care, but as equal partners in care—as full members of the health-care team. Perhaps most importantly, a mutuality of hope must be facilitated. By so doing, those providing the care must accept all visions of hope, even those (especially those) that go beyond the usual therapeutic hope continuum.

Hope is not limited to health care. People long for community and connectedness in many areas of their lives. We often live at a great distance from our families, but try our best to stay in close contact electronically. We have hundreds of "friends" on Facebook, but no one living next door that we know well enough to ask to borrow a cup of sugar. Instead of conversations, we watch movies and other programs on our laptops or smartphones during our commutes on public transportation to and from work, or when we are eating lunch at a place that offers Internet service. We now shop online instead of interacting with others at the mall, and we have prepared food delivered instead of frequenting restaurants. Gyms and home exercise equipment have taken the place of leisurely neighborhood walks and conversations with neighbors. We can take online courses instead of attending classes in person. Telemedicine and telehealth are becoming a reality.

We may be the most connected population ever, but find that we still miss physical presence. We may be living in a period of pervasive loneliness, but counter it with extreme busyness. As a result, we fail to recognize or acknowledge how lonely we actually are. The size of our networks over-shadows their lack of true connection. Is it any wonder that we struggle to find hope in difficult times?

Added to these personal concerns is the fact that our society also appears to be facing huge hope challenges. We live with divisiveness and hate crimes. There are great inequities, with a vast underserved population that does not have access to basic needs like safe housing and adequate food. Our environment is at risk, and our infrastructure is crumbling. We are still engaged in the longest war in our history, and threats to national security remain front and center in our newscasts.

There is an acute need for hope and for communities of hope. Where does this change in hope begin? Anne Frank, a young victim of the Holocaust memorably said, "How won-derful it is that nobody need wait a single moment before starting to improve the world." You can begin today. Become more mindful of hope. Be part of "hope-giving" as often as you can. Find a group or cause that needs your involvement and volunteer. Don't just give a few dollars online through crowdfunding (even though that is important too), but actu-ally show up. Interact. Support. Care. Build communities of hope. And then build some more.

The former Associate Justice of the Supreme Court, Sandra Day O'Connor, once said, "We don't accomplish anything in this world alone—whatever happens is the result of all the weavings of individual threads from one to another that creates something." Many cultures echo this thought by claiming our lives are joined together with a single red thread of fate. Perhaps, instead of a red thread, it is a bright yellow ribbon of hope.

Always, always choose hope.

Hope Highlights

- Hope is not just a personal resource; hope is best when done together.
- Many people long for community and personal connection.
- Patient-centered care needs to include hope-centered care.
- No community is more important than one that provides hope.

CHAPTER ELEVEN

Using the Power of Hope

Weeping may endure for a night,
but joy cometh in the morning.
—Psalm 30:5

There are many well-known and highly admired individuals who have provided insight into the concept, utility, and importance of hope. They themselves found and used hope to survive personal hardship, to support others in similar situations, or to bring about positive change in the world. This is evidenced by those who have personally faced and overcome great obstacles and adversity and have used their experiences to inspire others. Their writings and spoken words have served as beacons of hope around the world.

One well-known example is Nelson Mandela (1918–2013), the former president of South Africa, who was imprisoned for twenty-seven years due to political dissent in his country. Despite years of hardship and lack of freedom,

Mandela emphasized the role that hope played in his survival. His words continue to send a message of encouragement to others around the world: "Hope is a powerful weapon, and one no power on earth can deprive you of."

A similar example is Václav Havel (1936–2011), the last president of Czechoslovakia and the first president of the Czech Republic. Havel was a political activist who spent forty years opposing communism and working for human rights. He differentiated true hope from simply being optimistic: "Hope is definitely not the same thing as optimism. It is not the conviction that something will turn out well, but the certainty that something makes sense, regardless of how it turns out."

Meaningful and enduring messages about hope are not limited to great men. Many women, from both ancient and more modern times, have made equally important statements based on their religious beliefs and actions.

In earlier times, women who devoted their lives to the church were referred to as anchoresses because they were anchored to the church and to God. One such woman was Julian of Norwich (1342–1416). In addition to being an anchoress, she is credited with being the first woman to author a book. Her beautiful and hopeful words, which she claimed were spoken to her during a visit from Christ, still bring comfort and peace to people everywhere: "All shall be well, and all shall be well, and all manner of things shall be well."

A more contemporary example is Mother Teresa (1910–1997), a Catholic nun who became Saint Teresa of Calcutta. She is revered around the world for her devotion and work with the poorest of poor in Calcutta, India. She expressed her conviction that hope was an essential component when trying to meet their needs: "We want to create hope for the person... we must give hope, always hope."

Many other religious leaders have engaged hope when trying to effect positive change. Civil rights activist Reverend Martin Luther King Jr. (1929–1968) is one such example. Many meaningful speeches and quotes like the following are attributed to him: "We must accept finite disappointment but never lose infinite hope."

World religious leaders today continue to offer messages of hope that inspire followers to hold on, fight on, and not quit or give up when faced with oppression, life obstacles such as physical or mental illness, loss and grief, and adversity. Examples of three such hopeful statements are: retired Anglican archbishop of South Africa Desmond Tutu stating, "Hope is being able to see that there is light despite all of the darkness"; His Holiness the 14th Dalai Lama, Tenzin Gyatso, saying, "When we meet real tragedy in life, we can react in two ways—either by losing hope and falling into self-destructive habits, or by using the challenge to find our inner strength"; and the 226th pope of the Roman Catholic Church, Pope Francis, declaring, "This is Christian hope, that the future is in God's hands."

National and international leaders have incorporated hope into their personal and political philosophies and used these statements to bolster hope in times of trouble. Franklin D. Roosevelt (1882–1945) became president of the United States during the Great Depression in 1933 and served until his death in 1945. This was a period of economic turmoil and world war. Personal hope was familiar to Roosevelt as he had overcome the crippling disease of polio. His political task was to renew national spirit. Many people know his famous quote, "We have nothing to fear but fear itself." However, another one of his quotes about hope and the American spirit is perhaps even more compelling: "We have always held to the hope, the belief, the conviction that there is a better life, a better world beyond the horizon."

Other American presidents have been equally inspired by hope. President John F. Kennedy (1917–1963), was elected to office in 1961. Kennedy was considered a gifted communicator. His often-repeated quote about looking to the future incorporates hope: "We should not let our fears hold us back from pursuing our hopes." More recently, a speech at the 2004 Democratic National Convention by Barack Obama—and then followed by his book *The Audacity of Hope: Thoughts on Reclaiming the American Dream*—presented a presidential campaign based on hope and change: "Hope in the face of difficulty. Hope in the face of uncertainty. The audacity of hope."

In addition to religious and political leaders, well-known celebrities help others find and maintain hope. An outstanding example is actor Christopher Reeve (1952–2004), perhaps best known for his movie role as Superman. After a tragic accident, Reeve was left permanently paralyzed. He became a model of hope and strength for individuals living with disabilities, and he used his celebrity platform to encourage others to remain hopeful despite personal adversity and hardship. His statement "Once you choose hope, anything is possible" has become a mantra for those faced with illness or physical limitations.

As you were reading the quotes above, you may have thought that these were all unique circumstances and remarkable individuals who exhibited great strength and resiliency. Perhaps you found yourself thinking that you are not a leader or a celebrity, that you are not as strong as they are, or that your situation is different, that you lack their resources, and you can't live up to their level of hope. You don't have to. It's your own level of hope that's important.

What is essential is that you find and increase your sources and reservoir of hope. It may begin as a tiny flame of hope, but with care, effort, and support, it can grow bigger and bigger until it warms your spirit and lights your way forward.

Hope Highlights

- Messages of hope have endured through the centuries.
- While personal situations are unique, hope has many common factors.
- Leaders use hope to inspire others and bring needed change.
- You can—and must—develop your own hope.

CHAPTER TWELVE

Hope for the Future

Of all the forces that make for a better world,
none is as indispensable, none so powerful as hope.
—Charles Sawyer

A myth is a story, often a sacred story, that presents some enduring theme of human experience. Myths frequently contain unrealistic or magical creatures, powerful figures, fantastic imagery, and impossible feats. Despite these characteristics, myths often have historical connection and contain some wisdom or warning. The myth of Pandora's box is linked to hope.

Many centuries ago, Greek mythology recorded the story of Pandora's box. Given to her by the Greek god Zeus when he sent her to be the first woman on earth, Zeus warned Pandora to never open the box. Curiosity finally got the best of her, and when Pandora disobeyed Zeus's order and opened the box, all of the evils of humanity escaped. All of the sources of trouble—like hatred, jealousy, famine, sickness, death, sorrow, turmoil, war, greed, and strife—were released into the world. The only thing that remained at the bottom of the box was the spirit of hope. The moral of the story is that despite the evils of the world, we humans have hope to encourage us.

This ancient myth appears to have been a precautionary tale, even a prediction for future societies. The evils that escaped then from Pandora's box plague us today. So how can hope help?

The Honorable Robert Yazzi served for over a decade as the chief justice of the Navajo Nation, the largest Native American group in the United States. When he spoke about the challenges facing our country and especially those affecting our youth, Chief Justice Yazzi warned, "All problems stem from a loss of hope." Whether focusing on our own nation or viewing hope more globally, we have to acknowledge that we are living in hope-challenging and hope-impoverished times.

Hopelessness is destructive, but it is no match for emerging hope. Hope is not only a powerful word and a powerful concept; it is a powerful force. The key to fostering hope for our world lies not in current circumstances, but in the combined wisdom and responsibility of individuals—hopeful individuals—working together to bring about positive change.

It is hope that forms the nexus between the present and the future. Writer, historian, and activist Rebecca Solnit, author of *Hope in the Dark*, wrote that "hope is about broad perspectives with specific possibilities, ones that invite or demand that we act." She further stated, "We don't know what is going to happen, or how, or when and that very uncertainty is the space of hope."

In the book *Hope and Dread,* psychoanalyst Stephen Mitchell notes, "New growth is embedded in old hopes." He also warns that old hopes are solutions to situations that no longer exist, and they will require transformation.

Henrietta Szold, who founded the Hadassah Women's Organization in 1912, remarked, "In the life of a spirit there is no ending that is not a beginning." She also said, "Make my eyes look to the future."

Transformation for the future requires leadership. A quote by President Harry Truman emphasizes this thought, "In periods where there is no leadership, society stands still. Progress occurs when courageous, skillful leaders seize the opportunity to change things for the better."

What conditions are needed, and which ones are already available to help us transform our old hopes, to create and ensure a hopeful future? Can we engage the collective power of hope, not just for sociopolitical purposes, but to better the future for all? Can we find the best thinkers in sociology, psychology, economics, policy, theology, business, medicine, and other disciplines and ask them to engage their own curiosities and to exploit that remaining gift of hope to meet not only individual needs, but the needs of society at large?

Hope—our hope—has the power to change situations and lives. We have the ability to lend hope and transfer hope to others. We can model hope, spread hope, and teach hope. We can become hope bearers and hope educators and leaders of hope. We can begin and participate in a much-needed hope revolution.

Author Barbara Kingslover, in her book *Animal Dreams: A Novel,* contends, "The very least you can do in life is to figure out what you hope for. And the very most you can do is live inside that hope. Not admire it from a distance, but live right in it, under its roof."

I would add that the single most important thing that each of us can do for ourselves and for others is to choose hope. Always choose hope.

Bibliography

Anderson, G. *The Cancer Conqueror: An Incredible Journey to Wellness*. Riverside, New Jersey: Andrews McMeel Publishers, 1990.

Averill, J., G. Catlin, and K. K. Chon. *Rules of Hope*. New York, New York: Springer-Verlag, 1990.

Baines, B. K. *Ethical Wills: Putting Your Values on Paper*. Cambridge, MA: Perseus, 2002.

Beck, A., A. Weisman, D. Lester, and L. Trexler. "The Measurement of Pessimism: The Hopelessness Scale." *Journal of Consulting and Clinical Psychology* 42, no. 6 (1974): 861–865.

Berzoff, J., and P. Silverman, eds. *Living with Dying: A Handbook for End-of-Life Healthcare Practitioners*. New York, New York: Columbia University Press, 2004.

Boerstler, R. and H. S. Kornfeld. *Life to Death: Harmonizing the Transition*. Rochester, Vermont: Healing Arts Press, 1995.

Capps, W., ed. *The Future of Hope*. Philadelphia, Pennsylvania: Fortress Press, 1970.

Clark, E. *You Have the Right to Be Hopeful.* Silver Spring, Maryland: National Coalition for Cancer Survivorship, 2008.

————. "Family Challenges: Communication and Teamwork." In *A Cancer Survivor's Almanac* (133–146), edited by B. Hoffman. Hoboken, New Jersey: John Wiley and Sons, 2004.

Clark, E., and E. Hoffler, eds. *Hope Matters: The Power of Social Work.* Washington, DC: NASW Press, 2015.

Clark, E., and E. Stovall. "Advocacy: The Cornerstone of Cancer Survivorship." *Cancer Practice* 4, no. 5 (1996): 239–244.

Doka, K., and J. Davidson, eds. *Living with Grief when Illness Is Prolonged.* Bristol, Pennsylvania: Taylor and Francis, 1997.

Doka, K., ed. *Disenfranchised Grief: New Directions, Challenges, and Strategies for Practice.* Champaign, Illinois: Research Press, 2002.

Dossey, L. *Healing Words: The Power of Prayer and the Practice of Medicine.* New York, New York: HarperOne, 1995.

Ferrell, B. R. *Suffering.* Boston, Massachusetts: Jones and Bartlett Publishers, 1996.

Figley, T. R., ed. *Treating Compassion Fatigue.* New York, New York: Brunner-Routledge, 2002.

Frankl, V. *Man's Search for Meaning.* Boston, Massachusetts: Beacon, 1946.

Gillham, J., ed. *The Science of Optimism and Hope.* Philadelphia, Pennsylvania: Templeton Foundation Press, 2000.

Gorer, G. *Death, Grief and Mourning in Contemporary Britain.* London: Cresset Press, 1965.

Greene, R. R., ed. *Resiliency: An Integrated Approach to Practice, Policy, and Research.* Washington, DC: NASW Press, 2002.

Groopman, J. *The Anatomy of Hope. How People Prevail in the Face of Illness.* New York, New York: Random House, 2003.

——. *The Measure of Our Days. A Spiritual Exploration of Illness.* New York, New York: Penguin Books, 1997.

Haight, R. *Spiritual and Religious Explorations for Seekers.* Maryknoll, New York: Orbis Books, 2016.

Harwell, A. *Ready to Live: Prepared to Die.* Wheaton, Illinois: Shaw Books, 2000.

Herth, K. "Abbreviated Instrument to Measure Hope: Development and Psychometric Evaluation." *Journal of Advanced Nursing* 10 (1992): 1251–1259.

Hickman, M. W. *Healing after Loss.* New York, New York: William Morrow, 2002.

Hirschfelder, A., and P. Molin. *The Encyclopedia of Native American Religions.* New York, New York: MJF Books, 1992.

Hodges, S. J., and K. Leonard. *Grieving with Hope: Finding Comfort as You Journey through Loss.* Grand Rapids, Michigan: BakerBooks, 2011.

Hoffler, E., and E. Clark, eds. *Social Work Matters: The Power of Linking Policy and Practice.* Washington, DC: NASW Press, 2012.

Jaffe, H., J. Rudin, and M. Rudin. *Why Me? Why Anyone?* Lanham, Maryland: Jason Aronson Publishers, 1995.

Jevne, R., and J. Miller. *Finding Hope: Ways to See Life in a Brighter Light.* Fort Wayne, IN: Willowgreen Publishers, 1999.

Johnson, J., and M. McGee, eds. *How Different Religions View Death and Afterlife.* Philadelphia, Pennsylvania: Charles Press, 1991.

Katz, R. S., and T. A. Johnson, eds. *When Professionals Weep.* New York, New York: Routledge, 2006.

Kingslover, B. *Animal Dreams: A Novel.* New York, New York: Harper Perennial, 2013.

Korner, I. "Hope as a Method of Coping." *Journal of Consulting and Clinical Psychology*, 34, no. 2 (1970): 134–137.

Kübler-Ross, E. *Death: The Final Stage of Growth.* Englewood Cliffs, New Jersey: Prentice-Hall, Inc., 1975.

Lama, D., D. Tutu, and D. Abrams. *The Book of Joy.* New York, New York: Avery, 2016.

Lindemann, E. "Symptomatology and Management of Acute Grief." *American Journal of Psychiatry* 101 (1944): 141–148.

Lopez, S. J. *Making Hope Happen.* New York, New York: Atria Books, 2013.

Lopez, S., and C. R. Snyder, eds. *The Oxford Handbook of Positive Psychology.* 2nd ed. New York, New York: Oxford University Press, 2009.

Mandela, N. *Notes to the Future. Words of Wisdom,* 85. New York, New York: Atria Books, 2012.

McDermott, D., and C. R. Snyder. *Making Hope Happen: A Workbook for Turning Possibilities into Reality.* Oakland, California: New Harbinger Publications, 1999.

Mitchell, S. A. *Hope and Dread in Psychoanalysis.* New York, New York: BasicBooks, 1993.

Moore, T. *Care of the Soul: Twenty-Fifth Anniversary Edition: A Guide for Cultivating Depth and Sacredness in Everyday Life.* New York: Harper Perennial, 2016.

———. *Care of the Soul in Medicine: Healing Guidance for Patients, Families, and the People Who Care for Them.* Carlsbad, California: Hay House. Inc., 2011.

———. *The Re-enchantment of Everyday Life.* New York, New York: HarperCollins Publishers, 1996.

Murphy, J. "Managing Hope." *Illness, Crises, and Loss* 1, no. 2 (1991): 46–49.

Nierop-Van Baalen, C., M. Grypdonce, A. Van Hecke, and S. Verhaeghe. "Hope Dies Last... A Qualitative Study into the Meaning of Hope for People with Cancer in the Palliative Phase. *European Journal of Cancer Care* 25 (2016): 570–579.

Nowotny, M. L. "Assessment of Hope in Patients with Cancer: Development of an Instrument." *Oncology Nursing Forum* 16, no. 1 (1989): 57–61.

Nuland, S. *How We Die: Reflections on Life's Final Chapter.* New York, New York: Alfred A. Knopf, 1994.

Obama, B. *The Audacity of Hope.* New York, New York: Crown/Three Rivers Press, 2006.

Parkes, C. M. "Orienting the Caregiver's Grief." *Journal of Palliative Care* 1 (1986): 5–7.

Pipher, M. *The Shelter of Each Other.* New York, New York: Riverhead Books, 2008.

Porter, E. *Pollyanna.* Boston, Massachusetts: Page, 1913.

Renz, M. *Hope and Grace: Spiritual Experiences in Severe Distress, Illness and Dying.* London: Jessica Kingsley Publishers, 2016.

Rousseau, P. "Hope in the Terminally Ill." *Western Journal of Medicine* 173, no. 2 (2000): 117–118.

Scioli, A., and H. Biller. *The Power of Hope.* Deerfield Beach, Florida: Health Communications, Inc., 2010.

——. *Hope in the Age of Anxiety: A Guide to Understanding and Strengthening Our Most Important Virtue.* New York, New York: Oxford University Press, 2009.

Sexton, L. *Ordinarily Sacred: Studies in Religion and Culture.* Charlottesville, Virginia: University of Virginia Press, 1992.

Snyder, R. "Hope Theory: Rainbows in the Mind." *Psychological Inquiry* 13, no. 4 (2002): 249–275.

Snyder, C. R., C. Harris, J. R. Anderson, S. A. Holleran, L. M. Irving, S. T. Sigmon, et al. "The Will and the Ways: Development and Validation of an Individual-Differences Measure of Hope. *Journal of Personality and Social Psychology* 60 (1991): 570–585.

Solnit, R. *Hope in the Dark: Untold Histories, Wild Possibilities.* 3rd ed. Chicago, Illinois: Haymarket Books, 2016.

Stotland, E. *The Psychology of Hope: An Integration of Experimental, Clinical, and Social Approaches.* San Francisco, California: Jossey-Bass Inc., 1969.

Terkel, S. *Hope Dies Last: Keeping the Faith in Troubled Times.* New York, New York: New Press, 2003.

——. *Will the Circle Be Unbroken: Reflections on Death, Rebirth, and Hunger for a Faith.* New York, New Yotk: New Press, 2001.

Weisman, A. *Coping with Cancer.* New York, New York: McGraw-Hill, 1972.

————. *On Dying and Denying: A Psychiatric Study of Terminality.* New York, New York: Behavioral Publications, Inc., 1972.

Wolfelt, A. D. *Healing a Spouse's Grieving Heart.* Fort Collins, Colorado: Compassion Press, 2003.

Yazzi, R. "Life Comes from It: Navajo Justice Concepts." *New Mexico Law Journal* 38 (1994): 175–190.

Zuba, T. *Permission to Mourn.* Rockford, Illinois: Bish Press, 2014.

Notes

Chapter One—How Important Is Hope?

"Hope is the pillar..." Galus Plinius Secundus, known as "Pliny The Elder" (AD 23–AD 79), was a Roman author and natural philosopher.

Martin Luther (1463–1546) was a German professor of theology, a priest, and a major figure in the Protestant Reformation.

Victor Hugo (1802–1885). One of the best-known French writers. Author of *The Hunchback of Notre Dame* (1831) and *Les Misérables* (1862).

Johann Wolfgang von Goethe (1749–1832), a German writer, statesman, poet, and natural philosopher, was one of the most important contributors to the German Romantic period.

Jerome Groopman, MD, is a physician-scientist who writes about medicine, biology, and hope. Among other books, he is the author of *The Measure of Our Days: A Spiritual Exploration of Illness* (1997) and *The Anatomy of Hope: How People Prevail in the Face of Illness* (2004). Quote is from page 208 of *The Anatomy of Hope*.

Chapter Two—Religious Roots of Hope

"The sun set…" is from Ralph Waldo Emerson's poem "Character" in *Essays: Second Series, 1844.*

Webster's 1828 American Dictionary of the English Language. Online edition: https://webstersdictionary1828. com.dictionary/hope.

Unless otherwise noted, all biblical scriptures are from the King James Version (KJV) of the Bible.

Definition of a Christian is from Haight (2016), *Spiritual and Religious Explorations for Seekers,* p. 145.

Several sources were used for the descriptions of the major religions. One was an edited volume by Johnson and McGee titled *How Different Religions View Death and Afterlife* (1991). *The Power of Hope* (2010) by Scioli and Biller provides an overview of various religions and how they view hope. For information about Native Americans, *The Encyclopedia of Native American Religions* (1992) by Hirschfelder and Molin was the definitive source. Also, there are some excellent references to comparative religions online. For an overview of Hinduism, see "Turn to God—Rejoice in Hope: Reflections of the Hindu Tradition" by Dr. Anantanand Rambachan, a Hindu scholar from Saint Olaf College in Minnesota. Written in 1999, the article was retrieved from the World Council of Churches (wcc-org/wcc/what/interreligious/cd33-03.html).

For more information about the word *tikvah*, see (https:/www.abarim-publications.com/meaning/tikvah.html/).

For the brief article "What is Biblical Hope?" by K. Gallaher visit https://graceintorah.net/2013/10/26/tikvah-hope/. Also, an overview of the two kinds of hope used in Jewish thought can be found in an article called "Why Hope" by Rabbi Yisrael Rutman at http://www.aish.com/jw/s/48891352.html.

The quotes on hope from the Holy Qur'an are drawn from "Islam Teaches Us Never to Lose Hope!" available online at http://howtobehappymuslim.com/?p=422, posted February 4, 2015.

The Bible verse Hebrews 10:23 is from the World English Bible published online in 2000 (author Michael Paul Johnson). Derived from the American Standard Version of 1901, it is one of the few modern translations of the entire Bible in public domain. See http://ebible.org.

"Inferno" is the first part of the classic epic poem from the late Middle Ages by Dante Alighieri (1265–1321). Called *Divine Comedy*, it details Dante's journey through the nine circles of hell.

The Christmas hymn "O Holy Night" was composed by Frenchman Adolphe Adam (1803–1856), and the lyrics were written by Placide Cappeau de Roquemaure (1808–1877). It was first performed in France on December 24, 1847, by opera singer Emily Laurey. The English translation (the singing version) was done in 1855 by John Sullivan Dwight (1813–1893). The song has been recorded by many artists such as Bing Crosby, Perry Como, Andy Williams, Elvis Presley, Celine Dion, and Carrie Underwood.

Chapter Three—Symbolism and Hope

For a wonderful discussion about angels, see Thomas Moore, *The Re-Enchantment of Everyday Life* (1996).

To view examples of angel art through the centuries, see Chester Comstock's "Angel Images in Art History: An Angelic Journey through Time" in *Sculptural Pursuit*, Spring 2003, or visit http://www.artsales.com/ARTistory/angelic_journey/.

For a description of the Pillars of Islam, including belief in angels, see www.islamreligion.com.

There are many resources online that address the differences and similarities of the Star of David/Shield of David and the Seal of Solomon. One source of both the history and folklore is https://en.wordpress.com/typo/?subdomain=stjudasmaccabeus.

Chief (Si'ahi) Seattle (c. 1786–1886) is the best known among the Indians of the Pacific Northwest. Native to the Squamish tribe, he inherited the position as chief of the Duwamish tribe.

The website for *The Hope Tree* (www.thehopetree.com) provides a description of the origin and meaning of all forty-eight hope symbols used in the sculpture.

To view the Butterfly Garden of Hope, see https://hopeforbereaved.com/.

Chapter Four—Defining Hope: What Is Hope Anyway?

"Everything can be taken..." is from Viktor Frankl's book, *Man's Search for Meaning* (1946). Frankl (1905–1997), a psychiatrist, was a survivor of Auschwitz. He established logotherapy, a type of existential analysis that helps a person find meaning in life.

For a discussion of hope as an emotion, see chapter 2 (pages 37–49), "An Emotion of the Mind" in Averill, Catlin, and Chon's *Rules of Hope* (1990).

Pollyanna is a children's book written in 1913 by Eleanor Porter. A new release can be found on Amazon.com.

For a thorough overview of optimism, see Jane Gillham's edited volume *The Science of Optimism and Hope* (2000).

An overview of the linkage and importance of prayer in science and medicine can be found in Larry Dossey's book, *Healing Words: The Power of Prayer and the Practice of Medicine* (1993).

In 2002, a definitive article by renowned hope researcher Richard Snyder, PhD, was published. Titled "Hope Theory: Rainbows in the Mind," it appeared as the Target Article in *Psychological Inquiry* 13, no. 4, pages 249–275. The article includes the following definition from page 250: "Hope is a positive motivational state that is based on an interactively derived sense of successful (a) agency (goal-directed energy), and (b) pathways (planning to meet goals)." Thus, the goals, pathways, and agency definition of hope was established. In this article, he also challenges the concept of false hope.

Averill, Catlin, and Chon's *Rules of Hope* research in 1990 was based on analyzing maxims, proverbs, and 108 metaphors of hope that speak to the use of the term in everyday language. It also indicates that hope metaphors—the language of hope and its meaning—become part of the socialization process for children.

For an in-depth discussion about transcendent hope, see *Hope and Grace: Spiritual Experiences in Severe Distress, Illness and Dying* (2016) by Dr. Monika Renz. Dr. Renz holds doctorates in both psychopathology and theology. Also see www.monikaarenz.ch.

One of the first researchers to conceptualize therapeutic hope is Sherwin Nuland, MD, in his book *How We Die, Reflections on Life's Final Chapter* (1994), p. 233.

In the article "Hope as a Method of Coping" in *Journal of Consulting and Clinical Psychology* 34, no. 2 (1970), 134–139, Korner conceptualized the demise of strong hope structures (broken hope) in the following way:

1. The rationalizing chain becomes untenable.
2. Alternate rationalizing chains cannot be established.
3. The faith element of hope crumbles under the impact of internal doubts and/or external events.
4. The hope must be given up.
5. Attempts to confront the "reality" of the situation lead to no adequate and/or possible solution.
6. Pronounced feelings of despair associated with strong feelings of helplessness.

There are several versions of hope scales available for personal use. Measuring hope began with Ezra Stotland (1924–1993). He was one of the earliest social psychologists to show that a subjective term like hope can be included in scientific psychology. In his groundbreaking work, *The Psychology of Hope* (1969), Stotland noted that hope—*or an individual's degree of hopefulness—had become an almost technical term, an element of behavior that could be defined, measured, and applied in social and clinical contexts.* Since Stotland's work, numerous others have developed and validated ways to measure hope.

Psychologist C. R. Snyder, PhD (1944–2006), one of the most prominent pioneers in hope research, developed, tested, and validated *the Hope Scale* in 1991. The scale has been rigorously tested with more than 20,000 research subjects. It was first published in the *Journal of Personality and Social Psychology* 60, no. 4, pages 570–585. It is a self-report scale that measures hope rather than optimism. A copy of the scale and directions for scoring it can be found in chapter 2 of McDermott and Snyder's *Making Hope Happen: A Workbook for Turning Possibilities into Reality,* (1999).

Psychologist Shane Lopez, PhD (1970–2016), developed several hope scales. The Adult Trait Hope Scale is for people who are fifteen or older. There also is the Children's Hope Scale. Both scales and directions for scoring can be found in the appendix of Lopez's book *Making Hope Happen* (2013). An online version of Lopez's hope scales can be found at www.hopemonger.com.

Two clinical psychologists, Anthony Scioloi, PhD, and Henry Biller, PhD, (see *The Power of Hope* [2010] and *Hope in the Age of Anxiety* [2009]) provide an extensive online resource on hope (www.gainhope.com). It offers a detailed hope scale that is scored electronically. The Adult Hope Test has two parts. Part A (forty questions) provides a measure of your current or state hope level. Part B (fifty-five questions) measures your long-term capacity for hope.

Kaye Herth, PhD, RN, developed both a long- and short-report hope scale. The Herth Hope Scale is a thirty-item self-report. The Herth Hope Index is a shorter form of twelve items. It was originally published in Herth's "Abbreviated Instrument to Measure Hope: Development and Psychometric Evaluation" in the *Journal of Advanced Nursing* 10 (1992): 1251–1259. Both scales can be found online at www.allcare.org.

Hope researcher and nurse Mary L. Nowotny, PhD, RN, also developed an early hope scale (*Oncology Nursing Forum* 16, no. 1 [1989]: 57–61). Based on her doctoral dissertation research, she identified critical attributes that must be included for hope to be measured. The Nowotny Hope Scale has been used for assessment purposes in clinical settings.

It is also possible to measure hopelessness. See for example Beck, et al., "The Measurement of Pessimism: The Hopelessness Scale," *Journal of Consulting and Clinical Psychology* 42, no. 6 (1974): 861–865.

Greg Anderson is the author of a best-selling self-help book, *The Cancer Conqueror: An Incredible Journey to Wellness*

(1990), and the founding chairman of Cancer Recovery Foundation of America (www.greganderson.org), which focuses on cancer prevention and survival training.

Chapter Five—Maintaining Personal Hope in Difficult Times

"There never was night..." is by Dinah Mulock Craik (1828–1887), English novelist (*The Little Prince*) and poet. This quote is from "The Golden Gate" in *Mulock's Poems, New and Old*, 1988.

Soul retreat is a concept found in Thomas Moore's book, *Care of the Soul: Twenty-Fifth Anniversary Edition: A Guide for Cultivating Depth and Sacredness in Everyday Life* (2016).

For a comprehensive overview of the varieties of hopelessness and its impact, see chapter 3 (pages 69–94), "What Is Hopelessness?" in Scioli and Biller's *The Power of Hope* (2010).

The quote from former Associate Supreme Court Justice Sandra Day O'Connor is drawn from remarks she made November 4, 1994, at the annual conference of the National Coalition for Cancer Survivorship in Washington, DC.

Louis (Studs) Terkel (1912–2008) was a Pulitzer Prize–winning journalist, oral historian, and a storyteller, telling the stories of people in everyday life. He published eleven books, including *Hope Dies Last: Keeping the Faith in Troubled Times* (2003) and *Will the Circle be Unbroken: Reflections on Death, Rebirth, and Hunger for Faith* (2001).

Some additional exercises for better understanding the way you hope can be found in Clark's *You Have the Right to Be Hopeful* (2008).

A free program on learning and strengthening needed skills for dealing with a crisis can be found in the *Cancer Survival Toolbox: Building Skills That Work for You* (www.canceradvocacy.org/resources/cancer-survival-toolbox/). This easy-to-use program covers finding information, negotiation, communication, decision-making, problem solving, and standing up for your rights. A free audio version is available from iTunes.

Chapter Six—Helping a Loved One Sustain Hope

The Irish proverb used to begin the chapter was found in the book *The Shelter of Each Other* (2008) by psychologist Mary Pipher, PhD. Pipher discusses the changes, challenges, and realities facing families and communities today.

J. B. Murphy, PhD, was one of the first clinicians to describe the linkage of family patterns or family constellations to hope. See Murphy, J. B., "Managing Hope." *Illness, Crises, and Loss* 1, no. 2 (1991): 46–49.

To explore the religious framework for hope, see *The Power of Hope* (2010). Scioli and Biller provide an overview of religion's link to hope, sources of faith, and six ways of being spiritual. They also include several quizzes for determining spiritual types (pages 141–142).

For an expanded discussion of the importance of family communication and problems that families face during a crisis, see Clark, E., "Family Challenges: Communication and Teamwork," in *A Cancer Survivor's Almanac,* edited by B. Hoffman (Hoboken, New Jersey: John Wiley and Sons, 2004), 133–146.

Ellen Stovall (1946–2016) was a forty-four-year survivor of cancer who served as the CEO of the National Coalition for Cancer Survivorship from 1992–2008. She was a consummate communicator and a leading advocate for better cancer care. Her frequently quoted words, linking communication and hope, were published in an article by Clark, E., and E. Stovall, "Advocacy: The Cornerstone of Cancer Survivorship," *Cancer Practice* 4, no. 5 (1996): 239–244.

Chapter Seven—Finding Hope at End of Life

Hope never abandons you… is a quote by psychologist George Weinberg, PhD (1929-2017). See https://www.brainy quote.com/quotes/authors/g/george_weinberg.html.

In 1955, British anthropologist Geoffrey Gorer coined the phrase *pornography of death* to describe contemporary views on death. His research was published in *Death, Grief and Mourning in Contemporary Britain* (1965).

Elisabeth Kübler-Ross's groundbreaking work on dying was first published in *On Death and Dying* (1969). She wrote several more books on the subject, including *Death: The Final Stage of Growth* (1974).

An advance directive is a legal form that documents your wishes concerning medical treatment at end of life. Advance directives are legally valid throughout the United States, but each state uses a state-specific document. You can download a free copy for use in your state by visiting http://www.caringinfo.org.

Another important document is called POLST or Physician Orders for Life-Sustaining Treatment. POLST does not replace an advance directive, but it creates specific medical orders to be honored by health-care workers during a medical crisis. It documents a conversation between the physician and a patient who is approaching end of life.

A good resource for writing an ethical will is Baines's *Ethical Wills: Putting Your Values on Paper* (2002).

To learn more about what hospice and palliative care offers and to locate a hospice or palliative care provider in your area, visit the online site of the National Hospice and Palliative Care Organization at www.nhpco.org.

Chapter Eight—Reclaiming Hope after Grief

"In the midst of winter…" is from the essay *Return to Tipasa* (1952) by Albert Camus (1913–1960), French philosopher and author.

The characteristics of acute grief were determined in 1944 when psychiatrist Erich Lindemann conducted his classic study of relatives who had lost loved ones in the tragic Coconut Grove fire in Boston. His findings have been labeled "the symptomatology of acute grief." The topic was first published in Lindemann, E., "Symptomatology and Management of Acute Grief," *American Journal of Psychiatry* 101 (1944), 141–148.

"Give sorrow words…" is from the play, *The Tragedy of Macbeth* by English playwright William Shakespeare (c. 1564–1616).

Sitting shivah is a Jewish custom that includes a ritualized system for mourning and encourages the open expression of grief. See Johnson and McGee (1991), *How Different Religions View Death and Afterlife*. For Reform Judaism, see www.ReformJudaism.org/sitting-shiva.

Edna St. Vincent Millay (1892–1950) was an American poet. "Life must go on…" is from *Second April* (1921).

Chapter Nine—Restoring Professional Hope

To explore the impact of witnessing suffering as a professional, see Arbore, P., R. S. Katz, and T. A. Johnson, "Suffering and the Caring Professional" in *When Professionals Weep*, edited by R. S. Katz and T. A. Johnson (New York, New York: Routledge, 2002), 13–26.

The concept of disenfranchised grief is from Doka's *Disenfranchised Grief: New Directions, Challenges, and Strategies for Practice* (1989).

For an overview and suggestions for dealing with burnout and compassion fatigue, see Figley's edited work, *Treating Compassion Fatigue* (2002).

The quote by C. Murray Parkes, one of the foremost experts on grief, is from an article called "Orienting the Caregiver's Grief." It was published in the first volume of the *Journal of Palliative Care* (1986), 7.

"The new day is too dear…" is from *The Letters of Ralph Waldo Emerson* (1941), 439.

Chapter Ten—Building Communities of Hope

"It is impossible to find sufficient hope just in ourselves," is a statement by German political theologian Johann Baptist Metz, translated from German and quoted in Renz, M., *Hope and Grace: Spiritual Experiences in Severe Distress, Illness and Dying* (London: Jessica Kingsley Publishers, 2016), 59.

To review the historical moments of the HIV epidemic since its beginnings in 1981, see ADVERTing HIV and AIDS (http://www.avert.org). For an overview, "AIDS in the 80's: The Rise of a Civil Rights Movement," see http://www.cnn.com/2016/04/14/health/aids-atlanta-emory-university-the-80s.

Social work is frequently referred to as the profession of hope. *Hope Matters: The Power of Social Work,* edited by E. Clark and E. Hoffler (2015), contains fifty-eight narratives written by social workers that describe the role hope plays in bringing about positive change at all levels of intervention.

An example of a government regulation in health care is the hospice care insurance benefit for individuals sixty-five and older, which falls under Medicare Part A (Hospital

Insurance). Both your doctor and the hospice medical director must certify that you have a life-limiting illness and you are expected to live six moths or less.

"How wonderful it is…" is from a story called "Give!" (dated March 26, 1944) written by Anne Frank (1929–1945) and published in *Anne Frank's Tales from the Secret Annex* (1947).

"We don't accomplish anything in this world alone…" is a quote by Sandra Day O'Connor, former Associate Chief Justice of the US Supreme Court. Retrieved March 18, 2017 https://www.brainyquote.com/quotes/quotes/s/sandra-dayo372198.html.

Life review therapy, also called reminiscence therapy, is a psychosocial intervention frequently used with older individuals or with those facing end of life. Life review guides a person, in chronological order, through life experiences, allowing time for review and evaluation. Its purpose is to find meaning and acceptance in one's life. Life review can improve mood, bolster hope, and alleviate depression. Reminiscence therapy, along with the use of tangible prompts, is also used with patients who have dementia.

Chapter Eleven—Using the Power of Hope

"Hope is a powerful weapon…" is from Mandela, N. (2012), page 85.

"Hope is definitely not the same thing as optimism…" is a quote by Václav Havel. See https://en.wikiquote.org/wiki/Václav_Havel.

"All shall be well…" is a quote by Julian of Norwich. See https://www.christianhistoryinstitute.org/incontext/article/julian/.

"We want to create hope…" is a quote by Saint Teresa of Calcutta. See http://www.azquotes.com/quote/685912.

"We must accept finite disappointment…" is a quote by the Reverend Martin Luther King, Jr. See https://www.brainyquote.com/quotes/quotes/m/martinluth297522.html.

"Hope is being able to see that there is light…" is a quote by Desmond Tutu. See https://www.brainyquote.com/quotes/quotes/d/desmondtut454129.html.

"When we meet real tragedy in life…" is by Tenzin Gyetso, the Dalai Lama. See https://www.brainyquote.com/quotes/quotes/d/dalailama621067.html, accessed May 29, 2017.

"This is Christian hope…" is a quote by Pope Francis. See *Pope Francis' Little Book of Wisdom: The Essential Teachings* (San Francisco, California: Hampton Roads Publishing, 2015), 14.

"We have always held to the hope…" is a quote by President Franklin Delano Roosevelt. See http://www.presidency.ucsb.edu/ws/?pid=15870.

"We should not let our fears hold us back…" is a quote from President John F. Kennedy's inaugural address, January 20, 1961, (https://www.jfklibrary.org).

"Hope in the face of difficulty…" is a quote by President Barack Obama. See *The Audacity of Hope* (2006).

"In the presence of hope..." is a quote by Christopher Reeve. See Reeve, C., *Nothing Is Impossible: Reflections on a New Life* (New York, New York: Random House, 2002).

Chapter Twelve—Hope for the Future

The title for chapter 12 is a variation of a title of a book from 1970, *The Future of Hope*. Edited by Walter Capps, it is a collection of essays that map the early hope movement of the twentieth century with the theme of "hope and its relation to the future."

"Of all the forces..." is a quote by Charles Sawyer (1887–1979) who served as US Secretary of Commerce from 1948–1953 under the Truman administration. See www. Izquotes.com/quote/350687.

"All problems stem from..." is from Yazzi, R. (1994), 177.

As noted on the back cover of the 2016 edition of *Hope in the Dark*: *Untold Histories, Wild Possibilities*, Rebecca Solnit "makes a radical case for hope as a commitment to act in a world whose future remains uncertain and unknowable." The quotes used for the text are from her preface, pages xiii and xxiii.

"New growth is embedded..." is from Mitchell, S., *Hope and Dread* (1993), 221.

Henrietta Szold (1860–1945) founded Hadassah in 1912. Her first quote, "In the life of a spirit..." is from www. izquotes.com/author/henrietta-szold. "Make my eyes look to the future" is from "Our History. Hadassah, The Women's Zionist Organization of America" (www.archive.hadassah.org).

"In periods where there is no leadership..." is from President Harry Truman. See www.azquotes.com/author/14817-Harry_S_Truman.

"The very least you can do..." is from Barbara Kingslover's *Animal Dreams: A Novel.* See http://www.kingsolver.com/books/excerpts/animal-dreams.html.

ABOUT THE AUTHOR

 Author, speaker, and hope advocate Dr. Elizabeth J. Clark is a health-care professional who has worked extensively with cancer survivors, those facing life-challenging illnesses, and those struggling with loss and grief. She served as the CEO of the National Association of Social Workers for over a decade and is a member of the Academy of Certified Social Workers, the National Academies of Practice, and the International Work Group on Death, Dying, and Bereavement. Along with her husband, she lives a hope-filled life in the Catskill Mountains in upstate New York where pine trees fill her soul.

CPSIA information can be obtained
at www.ICGtesting.com
Printed in the USA
FFHW021101130119
50163919-55077FF